Borderless Church

Borderless Church: Shaping the Church for the Twenty-first Century

David Lundy

Foreword by Stuart Briscoe

Authentic

11 10 09 08 07 06 05   7 6 5 4 3 2 1

First published 2005 by Authentic Media
9 Holdom Avenue, Bletchley, Milton Keynes, Bucks,
MK1 1QR, UK
and 129 Mobilization Drive, Waynesboro, GA 30830-4575, USA
www.authenticmedia.co.uk

British Library Cataloguing in Publication Data
A catalogue record for this book is available from the
British Library

ISBN 1-85078-646-1

Cover design by fourninezero design.
Typeset by GCS, Leighton Buzzard, Beds.
Print Management by Adare Carwin
Printed and Bound by J.H. Haynes & Co., Sparkford

This book is dedicated to my wife Linda, who gives her support to my writing ministry by knowingly sacrificing time that would otherwise be shared with her, and who graciously reads my manuscripts with an eye to their improvement.

Contents

Foreword

More than 40 years have gone by since Bob Dylan warned the world that *'The Times They Are A-changing'*.You may remember that in his song he advised senators and congressmen, writers and critics, mothers and fathers to get their acts together. He hinted at the dire consequences if they failed to start living with the new realities. I doubt if many people who have surveyed the last 40 years would disagree with Dylan that in his day the times were changing and that they have continued to do so apace for some considerable time.

In the church there are, however, many people who, while believing times change, believe equally strongly that truth does not. And accordingly these people are faced with an enormous challenge. How should they view their contemporary world? Firmly established on the solid rock of unchanging truth, bolstered by convictions that are inviolate, looking askance at many of the modern trends, they want to know how to react. Should they embrace the changes? Should they resist the changes? Should they run away from the changes? Should they rail against the changes?

Those who understand that Jesus Christ established his church prior to his departure for heaven and immediately prior to that departure intentionally commissioned the church as the vehicle of his ongoing activity through the indwelling Holy Spirit, do not run and will not hide.

Rather they look carefully, critically, and compassionately at the changing times and ask the question 'How can we faithfully proclaim and portray unchanging truth to dramatically changing times?' On the one hand they long to be relevant; on the other hand they deeply desire to be faithful. And the tension is telling!

David Lundy is well aware of the tension and has a keen eye for examples of irrelevance where relevance is called for and readily identifies unfaithfulness where it rears its ugly head. But he is more than an observer of the times. He is a practitioner and a teacher. For many years he has served as pastor, missionary, and church leader around the world. He has willingly embraced opportunities to interact with people of varying points of view, culture, and experience. The result is a healthy view of the contemporary church, a keen insight into the challenges she faces, and no shortage of practical advice on how she should go about being a force for change for the better in 'times that are a-changing'. His book, *Borderless Church*, is a timely distillation of many years of study and experience, and a portrait of his heart. It will prove helpful to all who want to be part of a church that lives intentionally and effectively in changing times.

Stuart Briscoe, Minister-at-Large, Elmbrook Church, Milwaukee, internationally-sought speaker along with his wife Jill and author of 40 books.

Introduction

What good is the kitchen sink if the drain is blocked? Some months ago we could not find the plunger to unclog the drain. Stagnant water sat in the sink overnight while we mused about where the plunger might be. When that failed, we bought bicarbonate of soda crystals to create a chemical stir in the pipes under the sink and poured buckets of boiling water down the drain.

A church that has forgotten why she exists is like a kitchen sink that you can fill but cannot drain. As the church rediscovers her missional roots in the God of the Bible and in her early history of spectacular expansion, the current malaise of the western-world church in a postmodern, religiously plural, and globalized world will dissipate. Remembering *why* the church exists will reshape the church of the new millennium and cause her to embrace simple but unobserved ideas, like 'you measure the health or strength of a church by its *sending* capacity rather than its *seating* capacity.'[1]

The church in the west today is viewed as largely irrelevant. In an age where the notion of *truth* or *absolutes* is scorned, the church with its metanarrative[2] defining reality is politely marginalized. The church in the west at the beginning of the twenty-first century proves her redundancy to society at large by incidents like this one: Absorbed by hearing the gripping Christmas story in a school for the first time, a London teenager asks his teacher about one thing that disturbed him in the story: 'Why did they give the baby a swear word for his name?'[3] To such a world the church better know how to relate, otherwise she will become an anachronism, like a European cathedral: all but abandoned apart from tourists.

The church in the west is marginalized

We got used to the power. And you know what they say about power corrupting. Until the fourth century AD, the church was the underdog, embattled, in a minority. Her influence on the fringes of society changed with the Edict of Milan in 313, enacted by Emperor Constantine, which permitted conversion to Christianity and required that church property seized during persecutions be returned to its owners. It took only the 24 remaining years of his reign for Christianity to become the state religion. Blurring of church and state roles became entrenched by such developments as the pope adopting the emperor's honorific title of 'Pontifex'. Priesthood and laity were separated, with political power increasingly associated with church leadership structures and offices. Thus emerged fifteen hundred years of privilege and status for Christianity, with religion undergirding the advance of western civilization. This system of state–church partnership provided protection and privilege that sucked the spiritual vitality and sense of mission right out of the church. The scriptural teaching that the true church should expect to be in a minority and thus driven to witness as a way of life was lost in the complacency produced by cultural acceptance of her trappings.[4] By 529, Justinian had made conversion compulsory. With faith not separated from culture or political rule, God's people lost sight that 'missions is the mother of theology'.[5]

The church became viewed as an end in herself rather than as a means to the end of fulfilling *missio dei* (God's mission on earth).

Summing up the gradual shift in attitude from 'the church exists for them' (for outsiders) to 'the church exists for us' (for insiders), as ecclesiology lost its biblical edge, Murray observes of Christendom

> The church's orientation was now towards maintenance rather than mission, and mission was carried out by specialist agencies, not congregations. Pastors and teachers were honoured, while apostles, prophets and evangelists were marginalised or regarded as obsolete ... The cross was less a reminder of the laying down of life than a symbol carried into battle by those who would take the lives of others.[6]

With the disappearance of colonialism and the de-Christianization of society in the western world, accelerating throughout the twentieth century, the church's unconscious smugness at her centrality to society ebbed, like a woodfire left unattended. In its place, there was an attitudinal shift toward missional church, as captured in statements like these:

> The day of the professional pastor is over. The day of the missionary pastor has come.[7]
>
> A ... form of ... Christianity ... can be characterized as cultural accommodation or even capitulation. Christian leaders and churches who choose this sort of response to culture practice a form of civil religion. They typically do not challenge people to enter a relationship that is tied to a radical faith in the person of Jesus Christ... Their evangelism strategy is guided by the goal of maintaining a 'presence' in the community, not realizing that mere presence in a religiously plural culture does not have the impact they suppose.[8]

> I say it's time we learn again how to be 'resident aliens',
> how to live out the gospel in every neighbourhood in a way
> that is understandable and compelling to our neighbors. We
> have to change the way we do church, because we do not
> live in Christendom anymore.[9]

Chapter 3 will reflect in more depth on the trend
and ramifications of the church in the west becoming
increasingly marginalized.

Migration patterns and rethinking of mission

Not only has there has been a power shift, but there
has been a demographic shift coinciding with the church
sifting through her own purpose and place. Churches
that used to be situated in middle-class Caucasian
neighbourhoods now find the world at their doorstep.
We are living through probably the greatest migration
in human history. Demetrious Papademetriou of the
International Migration Policy Program at the Carnegie
Endowment for World Peace in Washington DC
indicates that 200 million people, making up 3 per cent
of the global population, live in countries in which they
were not born.[10] Hence one discovers 5 million Muslims
in France, most of them being North African. Almost
one million Chinese are found in Canada, a nation of
only 32 million people. Indian restaurants seem as if
they are on every corner of British cities, not unrelated
to the massive presence of first and second generation
South Asians in the country that was former colonizer
of the Indian subcontinent. This aspect of a rapidly
reconfiguring world will be taken up in some depth
in Chapter 2. Suffice it to say here that it has caused

the church to rethink *where* is the mission field, and has reopened the church to the understanding that 'the world is its parish' – and that includes *here*, not just *there*.

The church has begun to understand her *borderless* nature. Eloquently, Hopkins, an Anglican pastor developing cell churches, describes this borderless, because missional, mindset: 'We need to learn new ways of seeing church. It is not the building; nor is it the institution. If we free ourselves from assuming church is defined by its *form and structure* and look instead at *function*, we might define church as 'a Jesus community of disciple-making disciples.'[11]

Not by accident have I titled this book *Borderless Church*. The concept was first used with respect to globalization by the Japanese management consultant, Ohmae, to refer to the impact of the wireless revolution in connecting economies worldwide.[12] It is similar to the image projected by the title of the recent popular book by Pete Ward, *Liquid Church*. Note what Ward has to say about why he chose this image: 'Its basis lies in people's spiritual activity rather than in organizational patterns or buildings… My main motivation for suggesting why we need a new pattern in church life: mission. Liquid church is essential because existing patterns of church fail to connect with the evident spiritual interest and hunger that we see in the US and the UK.'[13] Indeed, high time to discover anew the borderless, because missional, nature of the church.

Further accentuating this borderless conceptualizing of the church is the fact of globalization. Old lines of demarcation are rendered useless by the electronic communication revolution and its attendant social, cultural, and economic universalizing forces. Recognizing this, Friedman articulates: 'Thanks to satellite dishes, the

Internet and television we can now see through, hear
through, and look through almost every conceivable
wall.'[14] Borderless, indeed. We shall see in future chapters
how the world in which we live shapes how we perceive
ourselves and our institutions.

A globalized church has missional implications

Not only is the world shrinking in terms of where
you can find people of different cultures and religions,
but the numerical and power centre of Christianity has
shifted from the north to the south, underscoring the
global complexion of the church. True, Yemeni Arab
Muslims are found primarily in Yemen, but they live
in Sheffield, England, too. Alongside this trend is the
open secret that South Korea has sent over ten thousand
missionaries around the world. Before too many years
there will be more missionaries sent out from churches
of the majority world than from the churches of the
west, the first occasion for that statistic to be true since
the days of the early church.[15] Christianity has become
a global religion, but also the whole church globally has
become a *sending* church. Such trends are reshaping our
whole understanding of not only *mission* but *church*.
Again, the *borderless* essence of the church is perceived
as globalization makes its mark.

The made-over church

Uncommon it is for a woman to refuse a *make-over* if
she has the inclination and the money. Whether to
have hair restyled, nails manicured, and face wrinkles

smoothed by a beautician, or to reinvigorate body and soul at a weekend spa, that 'new look' is considered to be a necessity of life for many people. Similarly, the church is being made over, sometimes intentionally and other times without her knowledge. We call this *made-over* church a *borderless church*. Combining the sense of global and local focus in reaching out beyond her walls, *borderless* describes churches which have rediscovered their sending essence – a sending that is not a function of geography but of calling.

Some churches are discovering this self-understanding as a result of the changing world around them, whether that be in its postmodern or its multicultural aspects. Others are re-reading the Bible with new spectacles as the wind of the Spirit blows through the church in unforeseen ways. To help you put a face on what *borderless* looks like, four chapters in the book are devoted to demonstrating the theory found in these pages, as we look at specific churches which we could call borderless. These borderless or *glocal* churches come from three continents. Self-described *glocal* churches are a growing phenomenon, but only just emerging as we enter the twenty-first century. Although each of these churches is unique, there are certain threads that tend to be woven through borderless churches. Often found in them are these characteristics:

- Their theology of God determines how to 'be and do' church. Their perception of church starts with God as *sending*, *relational*, and *giving*. This theology will be explored in Chapter 1.
- Everything they do is viewed through a missional paradigm. Whether it is worship or discipleship, ministry is engaged in with both its *edifying* and *evangelizing* impact in mind. There is a holistic

approach to ministry with missiological convergence as the driving force.

- *Community* is intentionalized in a culture of postmodernists and immigrants where belonging is at its heart, as indeed it should be among God's 'called out' people. Community thus serves internal and external needs. Church becomes a goldfish bowl for those searching for meaning as defined by the supportive collective as opposed to the shrivelled individual. Guder has this understanding when he says, 'Many people ... view the Christian life from an individualistic or, at best, organizational perspective. Yet to be true to its divine mission to embody and proclaim God's reign, the communal body called the church is the central and foundational unit of societal life for Christians.'[16]

- Witness moves on many fronts at once: local and global. As churches learn from such biblical models as the Thessalonian church, as delineated in Chapter 4, they similarly conceive of global and local responsibilities in mission. Mission is a both/and proposition, not an either/or one. The 'glocal' church makes sense in a globalized world where borders have lost their meaning.

- Driven by the passion to communicate the gospel to a postmodern generation for which the concepts of absolutes and objectivity are passé, plausibility structures blend the objective (Scripture and the uniqueness of Christ), social (the church as a need-meeting community), and subjective (personal experience and media) that permit seekers to 'experience' truth. Read Chapter 5 to find out more about this aspect of borderless church.

Ecclesiology should be derived from missiology

So what, you ask? Why should I read this book? What is it saying that has not already been said? To be honest, I cannot really claim that I am saying anything new or revolutionary. However, from my background as pastor in Canada, missionary in India, Christian mission executive to the Arab world, educator of Christian leaders on four continents, and inquisitive seeker after truth, I bring interdisciplinary insights as to the purpose of the church which I believe have implications for the evangelization of the globe. At their heart is the thesis that the *church exists for mission, not mission for the church*. That perspective, contending that ecclesiology (theology of the church) should be sculpted by missiology (the theology and practice of mission), and not the other way around, is simply keeping in step with the Spirit, whose footprints in history we are to track. It is rediscovering the story of the Bible, that God has a plan to reclaim this planet, and that it is to do so primarily through his people, the church. As such, mission, as a branch of theological training, must be retrieved from its relegation as one aspect of practical theology to becoming a core discipline – alongside New Testament (NT) and Old Testament (OT) studies, church history, biblical language acquisition, and systematic theology. God graces and blesses his people not so that the blessing ends there; that mindset has helped produce a feeling that when we refer to *church* we are referring to places rather than people.

A little detective work in the Bible itself reveals that receiving the blessing is inextricably linked to passing it on. One example need suffice here. Forming bookends to Psalm 67, which is exhorting the nations to praise God, is this idea that God's people are blessed with salvation for the sake of the nations who are not blessed yet: 'May God be gracious to us and bless us, and make his face shine upon us, *that* [italics mine] your ways may be known on earth, your salvation among all nations' (vv. 1–2). 'God will bless us, *and* [italics mine] all the ends of the earth will fear him' (v. 7).[17] Church and mission: the two go together like oxygen and breathing.

The Rosetta stone of the church

Imagine the ripple that went through archaeology and near eastern studies when hieroglyphics were deciphered after the Rosetta stone was discovered. I have gazed on this incredible archaeological find several times in the British Museum. For the first time, on this ancient stone was found the same text in Egyptian, Greek, and hieroglyphics. As translations of the Greek and Egyptian were compared, the hieroglyphic alphabet was decoded and what had hitherto been puzzling became clear.

Likewise, as we wonder what the true meaning of church is when there is no *one* definition of her in the Bible, but 96 NT images describing her, *mission* becomes the church's Rosetta stone, the key to understanding her nature and purpose.[18] If we put our money on one image of the church (e.g. the bride of Christ) as being sufficient to accurately encapsulate the church's essence, we are looking in the wrong place for the model that drives the church's purpose.[19] In the storyline of God's rescue mission to planet earth, not in the metaphors describing the church, we find the overarching meaning and purpose of church.

A special word of thanks goes to Graham Jefferson, my pastor, for his helpful critiquing of my manuscript.

1. God as Missionary Desires a Borderless Church

Fundamental to reconciling ourselves to mission being more than a church programme, like hospital visitation or the choir, is rediscovering that mission is integral to God's reclamation purposes for fallen humanity. Mission is 'the central biblical theme describing the purpose of God's action in human history'.[1] Since *missionary* derives from the Latin for the NT Greek term, *apostolos*, meaning *sent one*, it is not hard to grasp that God is called a missionary God. After all, he *sent* his Son into the world. Nor should it be difficult to discern that the church is more than the *sender* of certain individuals called to cross-cultural witness, which we have traditionally understood missionary work to require, but she herself *is sent*.

Understanding God is at stake in deciphering mission

Even more basic to understanding *mission* is asking why God chose to restore a broken humanity. It takes us to the very heart of God's nature. If all theology is rooted in *Theos*, that is, *God*, then our *theo*logy of mission should be consistent with God's attributes. We see mission being the overflow of God's self-giving, relational, and compassionate nature. God was not unintentional about sending his Son. He was not an afterthought. Nor are these aspects of his character unrelated to others.

When we speak of the self-sufficiency of God, we are saying that he did not need to create us or the universe. The three persons of the godhead were complete and fully satisfied within themselves. He did not need to create humankind. But the act of creation and the inspired explanation of that (Gen. 1 and 2) hint at a sharing, a self-giving already present in the godhead, now springing forth in love.[2] Newbigin lucidly puts it this way: 'God, as he is revealed to us in the gospel, is not a monad. Interpersonal relatedness belongs to the very being of God ... No one can be made whole except by being restored to the wholeness of that being-in-relatedness for which God made us and which is the image of that being-in-relatedness which is the being of God himself.'[3]

Being made in the image of God, Adam became capable of loving his creator in return, in the same interactive way that love overflowed between the persons of the godhead. When that fellowship between God and humankind was broken at the fall, the father-heart of God did what it took to restore joyful divine-human union. This required a mission: first and most importantly sending his Son to planet earth, and then sending the church into the world. Hence the simple but profound words of Jesus: 'As the Father has sent me, I am sending you' (Jn. 20:21). Our being sent out to proclaim the good news of the kingdom is predicated, then, on the same commissioning of the Son by the Father.

I was astounded by learning from David Bosch's magisterial treatise on mission, *Transforming Mission*, that the term *mission* was not used the way we do in modern parlance until the sixteenth century, by the Jesuits. Instead, it had been used hitherto with reference to the Trinity, to explain the sending by the Father of the Son, and of the Holy Spirit by the Father and the Son.[4] Just as the Father was in Christ reconciling the world to himself (2 Cor. 5:19), the church rallies and works together to reach the unreached (2 Cor. 5:20). The sending has to do with love, the love rooted in God's nature, reaching out beyond the mutuality of the Trinity. This seeking of community by God in turn leads church leaders to say things like, 'The *life* of the church is found in the Trinitarian nature of God … another way to say that God is Trinity is to say God is community.'[5]

Is not one of the proofs of our conversion the fact that the love of God has been shed abroad in our hearts by the Holy Spirit (Rom. 5:8)? That's why those who have been healed and sealed with God's redeeming love, intuitively (and as a result of explicit instructions), seek to introduce that restorative Presence (1 Jn. 2:20) to those devoid of that transforming experience. A lengthy conversation I had with an Indian Muslim in Kensington Gardens in London springs to mind in this regard. He ended up explicitly telling me that while he was born a Muslim, with Islam's tightly prescribed view of God, he was really agnostic because he could not prove or disprove that God exists, having had no experience of him. Essentially what separated the two of us was the inner witness I had of the reality of Jesus, pointing to the fact that there is a God who is knowable (Rom. 8:16). In this new paradigm of the church, she exists, that is, she edifies herself, she is motivated in all that she does for the sake of those not yet in the fold. As Bosch eloquently attests: 'It has become impossible to talk about the church without at the same time talking about mission. One can no longer talk about the church *and* mission, only about the mission *of* the church.'[6]

Not only does God have a missionary heart, but he lavishes love on his creation. God is relational and therefore the church, in order to truly fulfil her mission, must reflect that relational richness within her communal life. The *koinonia* of the early church must be part of her present-day DNA too (Acts 2:42, 44–47) if she is to be missional. Counter culturally, the church must be up close and personal if she is to be evangelistically significant. Newbigin puts it this way

> The deepest root of the contemporary malaise of Western culture is an individualism which denies the fundamental reality of our human nature as given by God – namely that we grow into true humanity only in relationships of faithfulness and responsibility toward one another. The local congregation is called to be, and by the grace of God often is, such a community of mutual responsibility. When it is, it stands in the wider community of the neighborhood and the nation not primarily as the promoter of programs for social change (although it will be that) but primarily as itself the foretaste of a different social order.[7]

The story of the New Testament is missional

We need to look at the NT with fresh eyes that help us see the story-line more clearly. Think of Luke and Acts as a defence of the gospel to the Gentile world, rather than as a history lesson about the early church and the life of Christ. Realize that Matthew closed his book with the Great Commission of Jesus to go and make disciples of all nations, since it was his *raison d'etre* for writing the book in the first place. Clues as to this purpose lying behind the first gospel include not only the stirring conclusion to the book, but the increasing use of *panta ta ethne* ('to every people') toward the end (24:9, 14; 25:32;

28:19) as the mission to the Gentile world comes into strategic focus.[8]

What is the story-line we are seeing? It is that the church is more than *the sender* (the popular notion these days for churches that lay claim to being mission-minded) but *the sent*. The church therefore does not build herself up for the sake of her members but for the sake of the unchurched. Is this not the thrust of 1 Peter 2:9: 'But you are a chosen people, a royal priesthood, a holy nation, a people belonging to God, *that* [italics added] you may declare the praises of him who called you out of darkness into his wonderful light.'

It is an emphasis already there in the OT. The promised blessing given Abraham was for all nations, not only his blood descendants. Israel was redeemed that the surrounding nations might flock to her, discovering through her the true and living God; when the Israelites turned inward and elitist, they were punished, graphically told in the story of Jonah's refusal at first to witness to Nineveh. If the Scripture is viewed in this missional light, it has been suggested that it might be more accurate to refer to the Bible 'as the Acts of God rather than call it the Word of God'.[9]

The church is not the destination, but is on a pilgrimage

Entering the twenty-first century, the church will see her pilgrim nature, not only because of her marginalization to the fringes of society, but because this is how she should be thinking of herself anyway, as *ekklesia*, God's called-out people (Mt. 5:10–12, 13–16). She is radically different from society, but she relates the gospel contextually and as seamlessly as possible to the world she inhabits. In the postmodern world, describing people coming to faith in Christ as on a pilgrimage has captured people's imaginations. However, even the word, *marturia*, the NT Greek word for *witness*, is revealing; it suggests that to engage in mission is to risk unpopularity, to alienate, at worst, to be martyred, which was found to be so true in the twentieth century, as it had been in the centuries of the first church, before she established a power base in society. Being in the world but not of the world requires a pilgrim mindset, which should not be hard for a people on a mission, who can 'endure hardship ... like a good soldier of Christ Jesus [for] no one serving as a soldier gets involved in civilian affairs – he wants to please his commanding officer' (2 Tim. 2:3–4). Or, as Callahan aptly phrases this missional attitude: 'A pilgrimage philosophy of life takes seriously that we are beings who live in a world of matter, space, and time. But a pilgrimage perspective does not turn this truth into a crass materialism or a preoccupied institutionalism.'[10] Furthermore, pilgrimage connotes discipleship, the following of Jesus after conversion, perhaps why the early church described Christianity as the Way (Acts 9:2; 19:23).[11]

Instead of being concerned with self-preservation, then, the missional church gives away her faith. There is no more poignant illustration of this than a church that finally reaches a comfortable size only to decide that because she is more concerned about multiplying her overall effectiveness, she should subdivide rather than erecting a bigger sanctuary to house and attract more people. As a result, the church makes a decision to send out a nucleus of key families to do church planting, realizing full well that they must go through the painful process of achieving a critical mass all over again in the mother church. Different from the homeless alcoholic, the church does not engage in pilgrimage wandering around aimlessly, but has a destination in mind. For now, she seeks to imagine what that destination will look like, the heavenly city (Heb. 11:10), the reign of God in his kingdom, but she is not yet there, nor does she pretend to be synonymous with God's kingdom. The church engaged in mission is a church on the move, in pilgrimage. She is borderless. She echoes the words of the sons of Korah: 'Blessed are those whose strength is in you, who have set their hearts on pilgrimage' (Ps. 84:5). The church with a pilgrimage mindset is humble and not triumphalistic, always in process and motion. She is looking outside herself. She is not used to borders.

Incarnational ministry equals missional ministry

Are we past the viewpoint that mission is done only 'over there', and not 'here'? We shall address in the next chapter how the changing demographics of our western world, bringing those from other cultures in droves to our doorsteps, adding to the challenge of what is already a largely post-Christian, postmodern culture that only considers itself Christian when filling in a census form, offers us a spiritual wasteland needing evangelizing. Aside from that sobering trend helping us to rethink where unreached peoples are found, we simply must reconsider how the early church was formed and even the nature of Christ's preaching of the kingdom. As we reconsider the form of witness of the early church in Chapter 3, we must think *incarnation*. The Son of God took on human form (incarnated himself): a quantum leap identifying him with those who needed his message of redemption (Phil. 2:5–9).

How powerful an example that should be for us seeking to be missionaries: mingling with those unlike us – whether in terms of the music they listen to, social customs they follow, or the language they speak. Jesus did not simply stand on a soap box at Hyde Park Speaker's Corner, as it were (although he did some of that too), but he associated with the disenfranchised, the poor, and the sinners in the worlds where they walked and talked. Thus he ate with Zaccheus, the despised tax collector. He allowed a prostitute to hang out with him. He made those 'poor in spirit' seeking the peace and joy he had to offer feel welcome in his world. Succinctly stated, transporting his example into that of the church, 'because the church is missionary by its nature, it always seeks engagement with its context.'[12]

While mission is 'over there' to the extent that the church is not formed in a particular people group and so the church 'where she exists' sends missionaries cross-culturally 'where she does not exist', mission is also 'here'; it is local, because the church is situated in time and space in a particular locality, and her missional witness and life radiates into that world as purely missionally as her witness 'there'. We are to be vulnerable, exposed, laid bare – in a word, incarnational – and that's why, wherever the church is found, she is engaged in mission. By her very presence in society, the church is missional.

Therefore, it helps her salt and light witness when her ministries are inward and outward looking simultaneously. Worship, for example, is an art form almost totally missing from society (unless adulation of musicians and fascination with sports and entertainment celebrities are in view). Hence a lavish indulgence in singing and extolling God's praises, and in making a habit in corporate worship of being deliberately thankful in specific ways for the Lord's answers to prayers, can only leave the unsaved looking on, slack-jawed.[13] In this vein, Guder maintains that 'our worship is ... the first demonstration before the world of our sentness, as we respond to God's grace in the good news of Jesus Christ.'[14]

Concomitantly, as God's people encounter him afresh in worship, it invigorates the church for service. I shall never forget the first Mission-wide conference in eight years that Arab World Ministries (AWM) held in 2003. There was an electric atmosphere as a worship band from the States and Wales led six hundred of our 'band of brothers' in Christ-exalting and Spirit-empowered worship. To say that we left there recharged to do mission as a result of the worship experienced at the conference is not an understatement. Father God tabernacling among his people as we worship him is to know his blessing in one breath and to desire to give away his blessing in the next. We shall return to this aspect of the borderless church in worship in future chapters.

One further thing to mention as we consider the incarnational dynamic of missional churches is to remark on the trend of churches getting into the act of directly relating to churches on the other side of the world. This trend in British churches has been well-documented in *Churches Going Global: Connect! 2*.[15] Churches around the western hemisphere are becoming their own mission agencies. Grasping the incarnational dimension of this style of doing mission in a globalized world, missiologist Douglas observes: 'Connecting ... local church to local church, across the divides of culture, race, ethnicity, and geography, is a radical act of participation in God's ongoing incarnation. This local church direct participation in various mission projects throughout the global church allows for a new level of incarnational living.'[16]

A further application of the incarnational principle inherent in mission is that the gospel involves fulfilling the Great Commission (Mt. 28:16–20) and the Great Commandment (Lk. 4:18–19; cf. Jn. 13:34). That is to say, just as Jesus identified with the suffering and down-trodden, as well as calling high and mighty sinners to repentance, the church in the world engaged in mission will necessarily marry the social and the evangelistic dimensions of her witness.[17]

We are blessed in order to bless

The rediscovery of the Abrahamic covenant as being the OT foreshadowing of the Great Commission of the NT also hints at the ultimate purpose of the church: to be the means to an end, not an end in herself, that is, to bless the nations. The blessing Abraham received (Gen. 12:2) as he was called missionally to 'leave your country, your people and your father's household and go to the land I will show you' (Gen. 12:1), had as its end result 'all peoples on earth will be blessed through you' (Gen. 12:3). Israel received God's favour, his covenantal blessings, not to hoard like some nuclear stockpile, but to be a global blessing in turn (Gen. 17:1–4). The same Lord who came preaching the good news of the kingdom to the poor and broke down the dividing wall between Jew and Gentile through his reconciling death on the cross (Eph. 2:11–21) had, in earlier times, elected Israel to welcome the alien into their midst, to defend the fatherless, in effect, bless with God's covenantal love all who would receive it. Christ Jesus came into the world to save sinners, not the self-righteous (Mt. 11:19).

Perhaps the fundamental difference between the *missio dei* in the OT and the NT is that in the former case witness was centripetal (the nations came to Israel to discover the true and living God) whereas in the latter case it was centrifugal (the church goes out to the nations). In both situations, God's people were meant to see beyond themselves to Yahweh's larger purposes for the world. Tragically, this *raison d'etre* for God's chosen people has been lost sight of more often than not. Callahan scathingly captures this great omission: 'God sent his only Son to save the world, not the church.'[18]

In a self-absorbed and selfish world, it is hard for the church to escape the vortex of 'what's in it for me', of reading the Bible essentially for its promises and blessings (e.g. focusing on the one 'fear not' promise for every day of the year) rather than letting it speak for itself in context. Hence, for instance, we may be startled to find that Paul's rehearsing of the 'surpassing greatness of knowing Christ Jesus' and the joy of knowing him and 'the power of his resurrection' (Phil. 3:8–10) is actually the bungee jump platform for leaping into greater ministry opportunities (vv. 12–14). We are called to serve as much as we are called to be saved. We are not the end point of salvation but the starting point. Sadly, in too many testimony times in church services, we hear well-established Christians still retelling their conversion story – as if the Lord had done nothing in their life since, or as if there was nothing else worth telling. Christianity thereupon becomes ancient history rather than current events. Says one theologian, 'the "classical" emphasis upon salvation benefits as the reason for God's calling people to be his witnesses is contrary to Scripture and must be rejected.'[19] Laid out more bluntly and radically is Bonhoeffer's statement in his *Letters and Papers from Prison*: 'The Church is her true self only when she exists for humanity.'[20]

Putting a practical face on what we mean here, take leadership. Having myself been a pastor in two churches,

I am quite aware of the tendency of many church leaders to be unconsciously self-serving, to be the greatest hindrance to the local church being mission-focused. The pastor's energies and attention instead are devoted to committee meetings (often to service the church property), and jam-packed schedules of counselling sessions and services for church members. Mission, local or global, is an afterthought. Callahan speaks prophetically about the type of pastoral leadership needed in the church when he contends: 'We need an understanding of [church] leadership that is more proactive and less reactive. We need an understanding of leadership that is more intentional and less passive, more relational and less organizational, more missional and less institutional.'[21] Such leadership will put the focus on training, mentoring, equipping for evangelism, discipling, functioning as salt and light in the workplace, in other words, in empowering the laity to do the work of the ministry in the church and in the world. Not only are the many smarter than the one, and so a wider influence is felt in the community as the whole church is trained and mobilized, but the watching world marvels that everybody is 'somebody' in the church, that there is no pecking order that legitimizes service. The cell church has understood this decentralizing of leadership well for the sake of being more effectively missional: involving every child of God is in the DNA of true mission.

Not a popular message, this one of it being 'more blessed to give than to receive'. However, a materialistic and narcissist church needs to face up to the way that the world has squeezed her into its mould, repent, and rekindle her missional fires.

Conclusion

Headed to Canada to speak in some churches, I once had the opportunity to sit beside a Pakistani Muslim on the flight from Heathrow. I knew what his religion was because of the traditional white pyjamas and beard he was wearing. Knowing that Muslims did not consider it a personal affront to talk about religion with strangers, I decided to find out if he wanted to talk about spiritual things by asking him directly if he were Pakistani and if so, did that mean that he was a Muslim. He smiled and blurted out, 'You have me figured out right.' He went on to say, 'But I am a Canadian and live in Winnipeg, even though I have been in Pakistan for the past two years.'

'That's interesting,' I responded. 'My father was born in Winnipeg and I myself am Canadian, but living now in the UK. Why, might I ask,' I went on to enquire, 'were you the last couple of years in Pakistan?'

'I wanted to see for myself if Islam worked when the Shariah Law was practised,' he went on to say, 'but the fundamentalists are self-serving. I've been disappointed by the west and the east. What's wrong with the world?'

Stunned at this candour and spiritual insight as to the fallenness of the human race, I savoured the moment – before plunging into a prolonged discussion with him about my faith and assessment of the human condition apart from Christ. Sometimes, I guess, we forget how desperate the world is for answers, for a knight to come along in shining armour, which indeed has happened, in the person of the Lord Jesus Christ. Why, then, are we so silent (and I look guiltily at my own track record as I pen these words)? Could it be that we have been so conditioned to think of salvation in terms of how it benefits us that we miss the 'big picture' of being saved in order to be sent? God as missionary desires a church that is missional.

2. Western-World Cities of Masala and Chips

In the years before moving to my ancestral homeland of England, I pastored a church in downtown Toronto, designated by the United Nations as the most international city in the world, with 189 languages spoken and 51 per cent of its 3.5 million people coming from non-Anglo-Saxon backgrounds. In my inner city neighbourhood, I bought my newspaper at a corner grocery shop run by Koreans. I got my car repaired at a shop managed by an Irishman, with Pakistani and Somali mechanics. My wife's hair dressing salon was run by a Filipino, with Chinese and Somali hairdressers.

No sooner had we arrived in the UK, several years later, than headlines screamed: *Chicken Tikka Masala, Favourite Food of Brits.* What happened to good old fish and chips? My wife and I faced culture shock in listening to Afro-Caribbeans and East Indians speaking with faultless British accents. (In Canada most visible minorities are first-generation and still speak in accents reflective of their ancestral homelands, unlike the UK, where immigration from former colonies has been in progress since the 1950s when labour was in short supply.)

But that's not the half of it. The world may have arrived at the doorstep of most world-class cities of the western hemisphere in the last three decades in numbers unheard of since the Exodus, but the emerging culture during the same period of time in those same urban settings has shifted from modernity to postmodernity. Chronicling these two phenomena – a changing demographic and a changing worldview – is what this chapter and Chapter 3 are about. Our emerging post-Christian, postmodern, and ethnically diverse western world begs the church to rethink what and where the mission field is. In the process, the church will rethink *why* she exists and *who* she is.

Global village in the flesh

Marshall McLuhan coined the phrase 'global village' to capture the way that, electronically, far-flung corners of the world were being drawn together in the same kind of close-knit way as a village, a place where everyone knows what everyone else is doing and is somehow connected. The world came into our homes through the television in the second half of the twentieth century. Similarly, we began to take for granted the instant access and communication that telephoning fashioned. Not satisfied with hearing voices though, younger generations soon learned to depend on socializing through text messaging over mobile phones or creating video recognition phoning experiences. There are enough mobile phones ('cell phones' in North America) to service the population in Great Britain four times over, we are told. The number of phone calls made around the world in one day exceeds the volume of all calls made in 1984.[1] The interconnectedness of the world is what has come to be called *globalization*.

What was not envisaged by McLuhan was that the global village affect would be *incarnational* as well. That is to say, not only are we wired to achieve interconnectivity while being physically dislocated from those with whom we communicate, but we increasingly travel or live in proximity to those whom only a century ago it might have taken months to reach by ship: people from races our grandparents would have only seen pictured in *National Geographic*. Let me, then, describe this new cultural and racial mosaic for you.

Europe

Most of the migration of the twentieth century flowed from the majority world (or south) to the western world (or north).[2] For one thing, between 1989 and 1998, the Muslim population in Europe grew by over 100 per cent to 14 million, to about 2 per cent of the continent's population.[3] Consider, through these demographic snippets, how relatively monocultural nations in Europe have become multicultural in one generation.

- With population growth in prosperous Germany in decline, huge numbers of migrants have moved into the country, chiefly Turkish, especially to do menial jobs. Turkish doner kebab has become the lunch food of choice in urban workplaces. The building of new mosques with traditional minarets is on the rise, from 77 in 2002 to 141 in 2003.[4]
- France, former colonizer of parts of North Africa, like Algeria, has 5 million Muslims, mainly made up of North Africans who have immigrated to a country whose customs and language they are familiar with. The spat over Chirac's preventing Muslim girls wearing the headscarf in school because of its religious symbolism in a secular setting has simply highlighted a simmering cultural clash in which Francophone society must face up to its multiculturalism or risk

more than cultural clashes. In a similar vein, the murder of Ghofrane Haddaoui, twenty-three, a Tunisian-born French woman, when refusing the advances of a teenage boy in Marseille, was the trigger point that sparked a French protest of violence against women as expressed within Islam.[5] Shockingly, many demographers maintain that a quarter of the population under the age of twenty-five is Muslim. If the streets in French cities now belong to Muslim young people, no wonder *les jeunes* is a politically correct way of referring to young Muslims.[6]

- The UK has over 1 million South Asians, according to the 1991 census, who make this land distant from the Indian subcontinent their home – most of them being Muslims, Hindus, or Sikhs.[7] Parts of some cities like Bradford or Birmingham resemble street scenes from New Delhi, Dacca, or Lahore, having been settled by South Asians. In 1993 there were four hundred thousands Sikhs and 180 gurdwaras (Sikh temples) in Britain.[8] Leicester, for example, in a population of almost three hundred thousand people, nonetheless has 83 Indian restaurants, 17 mosques, eight Hindu temples, five Sikh gurdwaras, one Jain temple, and designs on becoming the Bollywood of the western world.[9] In London recently, my wife and I saw *Bombay Dreams*, a smash hit musical which captured the collage of western and traditional values in the globalized Indian scene, and no doubt fuelled in its success, in part, by the huge turnout of British Asians.

- Amsterdam has a large number of Indonesians, helping make Islam the second-most practised faith in that historical bastion of Protestantism – a city of refuge or freedom of speech for early reformers and evangelicals like William Tyndale and James Arminius, but now as equally likely to be hotbeds for radical Muslims. The murder in 2004 of the Dutch filmmaker Theo van Gogh, allegedly by a Dutch-Moroccan Muslim radical, underscores the prominence of Islam in Dutch society.

- In jest, London has been called the capital of the Arab world because so many robed sheiks holiday there, Yemenis take up residency, and real estate in the centre of the city is held by Arabs (the most famous example perhaps being Harrods, owned by the flamboyant Egyptian living in Britain, Mohamed Al Fayed). The largest mosque in Europe is situated in London's Regent's Park, with an Islamic university alongside. About 1.6 million residents of Great Britain claim Islam as their faith.[10]

- Afro-Caribbeans and Asians now make up more than half of churchgoers in central London, according to Christian Research.[11] Kingsway International Christian Centre in East London has three thousand primarily Afro-Caribbean people swaying and clapping to worship on Sundays. Ironically, as British Africans and Caribbean blacks are actively reaching out to other Londoners, they moan that their faith is perceived as 'a black thing' rather than 'a God thing'.[12] An Afrikaans South African church in London, similarly, has over one thousand worshippers on a regular basis.

North America

For several years, as mentioned, I pastored the English-speaking congregation of a tri-lingual Chinese church in the heart of Toronto. While my wife and I lived there, it was announced that the Chinese had bypassed the Italians as the largest non-Anglo-Saxon ethnic group in this megalopolis. The Chinese migration to Canada over the last 40 years has been a fascinating phenomenon, now making Chinese the largest visible minority (visible from a Caucasian point of view) in the nation, with eight hundred and sixty thousand, 27 per cent of the visible minority population.[13] A sign of the times is that one of Toronto's most recognizable politicians is a Chinese-Canadian, Olivia Chow, that street signs in certain parts of the city are in both Chinese and English (this is true of other languages and sections of the city too), and that there are at least four distinct Chinatowns.

Not without cause, Australia, the United States and Canada have been called lands of immigrants. To put this cultural kaleidoscope in perspective, when just comparing these three nations of immigrants, it has been observed by a political commentator that 'in modern times, the magnitude of immigration to Canada is without equal. Some eight million newcomers have arrived since the Second World War ... About one in six Canadians is now an immigrant (or refugee); the US equivalent is only about one in fifteen ... Australia's immigration proportion is actually higher than Canada's but much less diverse and so less ambitious.'[14] Let's see how multicultural the North American versions have become.

- There are more Dominicans in New York City than the Dominican Republic's capital of Santo Domingo (around four hundred thousand), more Punjabis in Vancouver than any city outside the Punjab, and more Jewish, Irish, and Swedish people in the US than in any country in the world. Spanish speakers now form 30 per cent of New York City's population.[15]
- Soaring Chicano and Afro-American growth in the US means that the States' population may be more than 50 per cent non-white by 2050.[16]

- Until recent decades, most immigrants to Canada and the US were of European extraction. For example, in the 25 years leading up to America's bicentennial in 1976, the number of emigrants from the majority world increased from 11 per cent to 89 per cent of the total.[17] The largest influx of immigrants ever to enter the States did so in the 1980s with 90 per cent of them being of non-European origins.[18] Meanwhile, across the border, according to the 1996 census, 18 per cent of Canada's population was composed of visible minorities, compared to 6 per cent three decades earlier – most arriving from distant places like Hong Kong, India, Sri Lanka, and the Philippines.[19]

- Although some surveys put the proportion of Muslims in the USA as 0.5 per cent, others maintain that the percentage of Muslims now competes with that of Jews, about 2 per cent.[20] Authors of one recent publication claim that every day 411 Americans become Muslims.[21]

- The new immigrant population tends to settle in gateway cities or at least urban areas in Canada. Not surprisingly, the largest Sikh gurdwara in Canada is in Malton, the suburb of Toronto in which the international airport is found, often the entry point for immigrants and, incidentally, within striking distance of the Airport Vineyard Church of international renown. Of Canada's visible minorities, 94 per cent live in its 25 largest cities; in contrast, only 59 per cent of Caucasians live in those same cities (visible minorities make up 32 per cent of Toronto's residents, 31 per cent of Vancouver, and 12 per cent of Montreal).[22]

Ten reasons for the church to become more glocal

Given the globalization of western-world cities, one has to ask if the church will awaken to the promise and potential of a mission field brought to her doorstep. Or, will she still insist that the mission field has to be *there*? Here are ten reasons why the church, like Cinderella trying to get home before the hour strikes midnight, should seize the day and scurry to become *glocal* at heart before it is too late to respond to an unprecedented opportunity God has given her.

1. **Temporary Receptivity.** Anecdotal evidence and common sense dictate that new immigrants are open to the gospel in ways that they will not be once they have acculturated to their new surroundings. Sad it was for my wife and me to discover while pastoring the English congregation of a Chinese church in Toronto that some of the attendees we had in our home, including some very westernized, Canadian-born Chinese, had never been inside the home of a Caucasian before. Some of them would walk around the rooms peering closely at how we had decorated our walls and rooms. Seeking new friends when first arriving, and often vulnerable emotionally, when the need for bonding with the host culture is not met, newcomers eventually find people who speak their own language and retreat into their own cultural or religious communities. It is quite possible to live in Toronto as a Chinese immigrant and never have to speak a word of English. Here, then, is a receptive audience for local churches to polish their communication and relational skills on, one they do not have to twist the arms of to get them to talk

about faith issues, let alone fear the scorning of their message. The failure of western-world Christians to have a *carpe diem* mentality to these witnessing opportunities is captured in missionary Bailey's words: 'The sad thing is that these *kairos* windows of opportunity close after a while. Thousands of these uprooted immigrants are open to the gospel when they first come, but a few years after arriving in their new homeland, most become even more dedicated to their traditional religions unless someone has cared to reach to out them with the love of Christ.'[23]

2. **Influencing the future leaders of majority world nations.** The complaint is sometimes heard that Muslim terrorists are given easy access to specialized knowledge by being educated in the west that has been turned against the west. Yet one must ask how much such radicalized students are influenced for good by Christians while they are studying amongst us. The tragic reality is that few international students, in the UK or the US for just a few years, will ever visit the home of a local family, let alone a Christian one. International Students Inc., based in Colorado Springs, estimating that there are six hundred thousand international students in the US at any one time, sadly provides this commentary: 'Many of them will maintain only surface friendships with Americans, but most will never see inside an American home. Many are lonely, having left family and friends behind.'[24] Tragic it is that few Christian families ever bother inviting a struggling student to their hearthside for a festive occasion like Christmas (what a wonderful and natural opportunity to winsomely present Christ). Little wonder that these students return home often radicalized to their own faith system and cynical about anything western, to

become the political leaders of Sierra Leone and the doctors of Azerbaijan. In the academic year 2003–4 alone, there were 79,736 Indian university students in the US, 61,765 Chinese students, 40,835 Japanese students, and 26,178 Taiwanese students.[25] Moreover, untold numbers of these international students are from least-reached regions of the globe: two-thirds of international students in Los Angeles are from the 10/40 Window, a 'window' where it is estimated that 95 per cent of the world's least-reached peoples are found.[26]

3. **Virtually inaccessible and unreached peoples are within an arm's length.** Missionary visas have not been issued for foreigners to India virtually for four decades. While the national missionary force has boomed and now numbers thirteen thousand according to the India Missionary Association, there still remain three thousand six hundred relatively unreached people groups in India. Vast tracts of north Indian states, like Uttar Pradesh, which I traversed in open air and mass evangelism for three years, with the Ganges River meandering through it and home to the Hindu sacred city of Benares, are a spiritual wasteland, predominately Hindu and Muslim. However, now Canada's South Asians number about seven hundred thousand, making them the largest visible minority group, after the Chinese. As such, it is the largest unreached people group in Canada, needing pioneer church planting efforts. It is encouraging, therefore, to see the small Nawa Jiwan Punjabi Church of Vancouver go into the heart of the local Sikh community at Fraser and Main to evangelize on Saturday evenings.[27] Later we will meet Bramalea Baptist Church in greater Toronto, with a growing outreach of her own to Canada's fastest-growing

South Asian population. What marks her as being different from the homogenous South Asian church in Vancouver is that Bramalea is harnessing her South Asian Hindi and Tamil-speaking members together with her white members to attract South Asians in the malls and in the neighbourhoods. The point is that you do not have to go half way around the world to reach Hindus, Muslims, and Sikhs. Or, one thinks of the 2 million Iranians living in North America, coming originally from a fundamentalist Islamic country, and where there is only one Christian worker for every 1 million inhabitants![28] Surely today is the day of salvation for these Iranians brought to our doorstep.

4. **Friendship evangelism is the most effective strategy.** Many of these new immigrants come from highly relational societies where self-identity is perceived more in terms of the group (family, tribe, or nation) than the individual. In such a context, friendship building is a natural and understood way to discuss who Jesus is. As the former international director of AWM, Abe Wiebe, once told me in offering advice in how to reach Muslims, 'Follow the Arab proverb that reminds you that if you have room in your heart, you have room in your home.' Arabs are famous for their lavish hospitality. Now that generosity can be reciprocated by those whose love must be practised in deed, not just in word, and whose holy book commands the practice of hospitality (Rom. 12:13). Sharing food is a universally-understood language (Gen. 18:1-8). All you have to remember is to follow a few simple rules like offering no meat to Hindus or pork products to Muslims. We'll pick up on this theme more in a future chapter. The church is exhorted to give hospitality in Hebrews 13:2. An Arab proverb

goes, 'A house that receives no guests receives no angels.' Building friendship bridges, not barriers, does not require the genius of a rocket scientist.

5. **Learning about another culture helps you to critique how much your own faith practice is cultural, not biblical.** In one sense, I feel I got spoiled by my service in the Chinese church. Already acquainted with deference to elders through my six years of missionary service in India and my 16 trips there since, that respect reached new heights as I was invariably called 'Rev. Lundy' or 'Pastor David' (for the informally-inclined), in the Chinese church, in spite of my efforts to disabuse them of any sense that I should be treated as part of a spiritual elite. Just last week I got an email from one of our friends in the church who had come to faith in the college and careers group and whom I had the privilege of discipling, stating that his girl friend occasionally chided him with the comment, 'Now what would Rev. Lundy do if he were in your shoes?' To build friendships with those from Asian, African, or Latino cultures has a boomerang effect on one. What we thought was humility now seems like arrogance; individuality seems like egotism; hard work seems like less than our best; transparency seems like presumption; and independence seems like selfishness. Rephrased, as we are exposed to those of other cultures and faiths, we find ourselves asking how much of our faith is authentic and how much is simply learned cultural habits (Rom. 12: 2).

6. **Learning about another religion helps you to sharpen your apologetic tools as you come to understand your own faith better.** Engaging Muslims in conversation about faith, something they find as natural to talk about as we might the finesse on the football field of David Beckham, will drive us to dig into the Scriptures

about the Trinity as they ask how one God can be three, or accept Christ's prophet-hood but deny his deity. Our assumptions about the nature of reality will be tested as we choose to befriend the Hindu in our workplace and find that they do not separate created from creator, as we do, but are monistic, in fact may believe in the impersonal nature of ultimate reality, Brahma. Sharpened by being driven back to Scripture and writings in apologetics to get answers we lack at first blush, we not only become better equipped to handle those from other world religions, but we begin to comprehend how to counter the relativism and agnosticism of postmodernist, mainstream culture. According to the context of 1 Peter 3:15, being able to give good reason for the hope that is within us, it presupposes that we *are* witnessing. Skill comes from practice.

7. **A multicultural outreach will lead to a multicultural church.** Many models exist of churches that grew into multicultural churches because they reached those in their inner city or urban communities, a diverse population, as that neighbourhood changed in complexion. One such is Tenth Avenue Alliance Church in Vancouver, which revived from a low point of two hundred in attendance to eight hundred today as a result of the decision to allow ministries to reflect the nature of the community surrounding the church, that is, to become multicultural. Declares Ken Shigematsu, their senior pastor, about growing a multi-ethnic church, 'It's the only way an Iranian Muslim, a late-stage AIDS patient and a Japanese Buddhist can find Christ in the same community'.[29] It is estimated that there are one thousand multicultural churches in the US and one hundred and fifty in Canada.[30] Such churches are 'intentionally multicultural', and seek 'to

mimic the image of worshipers from "every nation, tribe, people and language" in Revelation 7:9'.[31] Good ones do not create a homogenous blob out of the cultural diversity, recognizing, as Hughes reminds us, that 'Galatians 3:28 is not about the destruction of difference, but about mutual respect.'[32]

8. **A multicultural outreach and church will enlarge your passion for the rest of the globe.** Too long we have treated 'home mission' and 'world mission' as competing mission ministries. A little research shows that when churches intentionally move on both fronts at once, thinking and acting *glocally*, a synergy is formed that prevents the piranha syndrome setting in, that is, where one programme feeds off the other. Now if you put church building programmes (the concrete and mortar type) up against mission programmes, you find a different story. When we look at the Thessalonian church's example in Chapter 4, we shall see how moving on both fronts at once makes a church vibrant and missional. The pulling no punches mission spokesman, former baseball umpire, Tom Telford, says it well: 'We teach what we know; we reproduce what we are.'[33] Therefore, we can expect that the lady in the congregation who discovers the heart longings of her Bahraini fellow student by befriending her will develop a passion for the spiritual needs of the larger Arab Muslim world of 300 million people, Bahrain being just one of 19 Arab nations. We must come to grips with the fact that without leaving Europe or North America, we are in a missional situation. Among other things, for the borderless church, this will require developing intercultural skills.

9. **Forming a theological response to cultural diversity will sharpen understanding of how to relate church**

and Christ to postmodernism. It would be incorrect to assume that the proliferation and tolerance of a multitude of religious and spiritual beliefs means that knowledge of Christianity and of Christ have not been heard; it would be more correct to say that the view of our Lord and Saviour has become distorted when viewed as just one more alternative path in designing one's own spirituality. In such a milieu we must sharpen our response to the plausibility structures of religious pluralism, called by John Stott and others the most critical issue facing churches and missions today.

10. **Understanding the world religions surrounding you will boost confidence to reach your own kind of postmodern people, now uncomfortably different.** As we understand the relativism of the Hindu down the street, we are not stunned or flummoxed by the 'that's good for you but not for me' of a Glasgow Generation-Y gothic reacting diffidently as we share Christ with him; the purple haired, purple lipped teen does not startle us and leave us speechless as she seems apathetic to the difference between feeling and reason because we have repeatedly visited the Buddhist temple in another part of the town, and processed their failure to distinguish between myth and history.

Conclusion

The Scripture urges us to love the stranger amongst us (Lev. 19:34). The NT word for this love for stranger is *philoxenos*. Instead of being *xenophobic* about a changing western world, we should see this as God's *kairos* time to reach out with the *phileo* love of Christ. In so doing, we are demonstrating what church has always been meant to be: a borderless, missional community. The borderless church will be in contrast to society with its different degrees of xenophobia. Whereas tens of thousands of civil servants in most western-world countries will single-mindedly develop legislation, passports, quotas, and spin to keep strangers on the opposite side of their borders, the borderless church must love the stranger (Rom. 12:13), the neighbour (Lev. 19:18), and the enemy (Mt. 5:44).[34]

Western-world cities are multicultural as never before. This fact was driven home to me by my wife's story of her hair dresser while we lived in downtown Toronto. Her hair-dressing salon was run by a Filipino lady, who, Linda discovered shortly after going there, was a vibrant Christian. A few months later Linda had her hair done there by a Chinese lady. Perceiving a tailor-made witnessing opportunity, Linda mentioned that her husband pastored a Chinese church. Not skipping a beat, the Chinese hair dresser said, 'Oh, that's nice. I became a Christian myself recently. My manager led me to put my trust in Christ.'

In future months, Linda returned to having her hair done by the Filipino lady. However, one day she had no choice. The shop was full. Linda got her hair done by a new hair-dresser. Ever the friendship-maker, Linda knew enough about Somali facial features to ask the lady, 'Are you from Somalia?'

Taken aback, the almond-skinned beauty blurted out, 'Yes, but how did you know?'

Linda added, 'I not only suspected that as a result of my world travels, but I would hazard a guess that you are also Muslim. Is that correct?'

'Not exactly,' hesitated the Somali. 'My Chinese friend,' nodding in the direction of her work colleague who had done Linda's hair in previous months, 'helped me to see that Isa Masih is more than a prophet. He is my Saviour.'

A Filipino leading a Chinese leading a Somali to faith in Christ ... in Toronto! In fact, many emigrants to the west bring a vibrant faith in Christ. The church needs to be missional and borderless not just because the world is coming to our doorstep, but because of the world that was at her doorstep all along. But that awaits our consideration in the next chapter.

3. The Chameleon World of Postmodern Culture

Just as a chameleon changes its skin tones to blend in with its environment, so western culture changes its values, fashions, and ideologies on an almost daily basis. An icon of this chameleon tendency is Madonna, who can be a mother writing children's books one day and advocating bisexuality the next. Or take Nicole Kidman, who has patched together her own designer religion: "I believe in a bit of Scientology, Catholicism, Judaism and the Eastern philosophies. I take a bit of each, I am a hybrid."[1] Welcome to postmodernity.[2]

Not without justification, the Holocaust has been called a harbinger of postmodernity.[3] Science was meant to provide the universal understanding of reality and progress, but the 'objectivity' and 'empiricism' of the Second World War Auschwitz experiments inflicted on the Jews only unmasked its moral bankruptcy.[4] Reason, pragmatism, and efficiency were denuded of their pretence of ultimate importance, much as the emperor in his new clothes. Disillusionment at the possibilities of modernity set in, like a Canadian pond frozen by winter's blast, waiting interminably for the thaw of spring to set its aqua life free again. Postmodernity says that 'the pond ain't gonna thaw'. There is no ultimate truth. All claims of a metanarrative – like the message of a Creator rescuing humankind through his son, Jesus Christ, which is the Grand Story of the Bible – await their debunking. A father of postmodern philosophy, Jean-Francois Lyotard, actually defined postmodernity as 'incredulity toward metanarratives'.[5] Science has its limits, we are told. Religious pluralism can be encouraged, but not religious exclusivism. Inclusivism and diversity are 'hot'; absolutes and 'true truth' are 'cold'.

While not being averse to using the mobile phones and DVDs that science has spawned, postmodernists ask how we can trust a theory of knowledge that threatens ancient marshes and the poor people dependent on them in the Euphrates delta of Iraq as global warming takes its toll. How can Christianity, we are challenged, that unleashed the Inquisition on Europe and the Crusades on the Muslim world, reject my New Age experience by simply declaring that God's love is experienced only through Jesus Christ? How can Islam, producing terrorists that destroy the Twin Towers and tolerating systematic subjugation of women, speak of being the final revelation of God?

Further proof that the west needs re-evangelizing

These are not the attitudes and questions of an atheistic fringe in the western world. They represent mainstream thinking, especially in Europe. Watching Angels in America on TV, I was struck by how this play on the AIDS outbreak during the Reagan administration, so popular on stage in the early 1990s, now having earned Golden Globe awards for its stellar performances by celebrated actors like Emma Thompson and Al Pacino, served at the same time to make heroes of those suffering the ravages and death throes of AIDS and to neutralize the religious conservative response to homosexuality (not that AIDS is caused by gays), as portrayed through the eyes of a Mormon. Interestingly, rather than demonize the moral absolutes of the Mormon mother in reaction to her son finally coming out of the closet, she is portrayed with long-buried feelings of compassion. Her theology is scorned but her humanity tells us that everyone has a right to their own beliefs as long as they do not infringe on the convictions of others. All that to say that the Punk Rocker shopping on High Street in Manchester to make her fashion statement, the hip hop enthusiast in the night clubs of Montreal texting while dancing, and the obese couch potato baby boomer in Miami are as far away from the knowledge of the true and living God as any Hindu from Mangalore, Muslim from Chad, or Bahai refugee from Iran settling in those self-same cities (and don't forget that in a globalized world the hip hop urbanite might just as easily be found in Mangalore as in Montreal).

But is the church in touch with this reality? Tragically, for the most part, the church has her head in the sand when it comes to understanding, let alone relating to, the culture within which she finds herself. Let's then do a quick survey of this postmodern wasteland.[6] Our purpose here is simply to set the stage for what a missional response to the western world might look like in Chapter 5, and then in the chapter on Mars Hill Church of Grand Rapids, Michigan, to see how one church has engaged the challenge of postmodern agnosticism and spirituality. Let us, then, outline the salient features of postmodernity, also throwing out the caveat that there is much in postmodernity to be appreciated and to give us encouragement as we go forth in hope. After all, who really needs the 'god is dead' pontificating of modernity when the acceptance of the spiritual realm is a given in our present culture? Moreover, who needs the extreme individualism that modernity spawned when today's youth aspire for community?

Distrust of the past

One of the hallmarks of postmodernity is its distrust of the past. Youthfulness is idolized in fashion, advertising, music, and sport as grey hair points not to wisdom, as Proverbs maintains, but to redundancy. One only has to look at something like the Saturday weekly magazine supplement to the newspaper *The Times* to see the disproportionate glamorization of youth. Society trivializes the past as being outmoded and passé. History is not to be trusted because it supports the subjective power agenda of its scribes. Irreverence for the past is apparent when one in ten Britons are convinced that Hitler is a fictional person while one in twenty thinks Conan the Barbarian was a real person.[7] Again the traditions of the past are shrugged off as people, rather than read hard-copy books, download material from the Internet and read it in snatches on PDAs.

Distrust of institutions and power figures reveals the antiauthoritarian bias of postmodernity that allows it to dismiss the past. So speaks Joel of Generation X: 'We have little allegiance to corporations or educational institutions. Many of us dislike big businesses that boomers before us made great ... Our most permanent address is an email address.'[8]

Deconstructionism is lauded as the new hermeneutic, that is, a way of interpreting texts and meaning in language which attributes all meaning to social contrivance, to historical and cultural conditioning.[9] Thus, for instance, the writers of the Bible, for the most part, are dismissed as white males seeking to retain their power base in society.

As indicated above, part of that distrust of the past is a sense of disillusionment with modernity. Modernity had bifurcated knowledge from morality, just as the atom was split to produce the destructive forces of the atomic bomb. Orwell's *1984* became more than a symbol of the dangers of materialism divorced from meaning, as scientific breakthrough resulted in millions of blue collar workers losing their jobs to robots and the vagaries of a mechanistic and materialistic world.

The absolutizing of relativism

Consider this. A decade ago a Barna poll in the US revealed that two-thirds of Americans believe there is no such thing as absolute truth – this in the land of the Moral Majority.[10] While the scientists of modernity admit the difficulty of isolating objective facts, postmodernists scorn the notion of unbiased truth; for the latter, accepting that there are no absolutes, only partial truths, or perspectives, is the most objective one can get. This view grew out of instrumentalism, a philosophy that assumes there is an external world discerned through our senses. It contends that we are not able to know when our theories of reality are consistent with external reality or only subjective projections. Hence, meaning is found in people's heads, not in some objective source.[11] On the one hand, this can produce an inability to stand for anything, a wishy-washy moral spinelessness, and on the other, an intolerance of any form of dogmatism, of any claim to ultimate truth.

Parodying this anaesthetizing of society through the political correctness of relativism, of extreme inclusivism, is the chatter heard on a Chicago radio talk show. Hear Dennis Prager carp about religious tolerance not being modelled in the American school system

> Liberals are always talking about pluralism, but that is
> not what we mean: In public schools, Jews don't meet
> Christians. Christians don't meet Hindus. Everybody meets
> nobody. That is, as I explain to Jews all the time, why their
> children so easily intermarry. Jews don't marry Christians.
> Non-Jewish Jews marry non-Christian Christians. Jews-
> for-nothing marry Christians-for-nothing. They get along
> great because they affirm nothing. They have everything in
> common – nothing. That's not pluralism.[12]

Another sample from the marketing kit of the postmodern
salesperson is the push to egalitarianism inherent to
relativism. For instance, in the academic sphere, relativism
rears its head in 'grade inflation', which pushes grading
for all students upwards, to 'A' or 'B' at worst, allegedly
in the name of equal opportunity, but in essence, having
the effect of grade equalization, lest anyone's perspective
be undermined as invalid or inferior. Or, take the radio
or TV talk shows, so popular in the UK and US, which
give equal credence to everyone's opinion. Even if you
are a well-read scholar on the topic under discussion,
your viewpoint is treated as having no more merit than
someone who is thinking about the subject for the first
time.[13]

All claims of ultimate truth, especially in religious
matters, are dismissed as *religious exclusivism*, and
subject to intolerance and censorship. Of the world
religions, Christianity, Islam, and Judaism (their non-
liberal constituencies[14]) would be so classified, with
Buddhism and Hinduism deemed as being within the
camp of *religious pluralism*. Religious pluralism can be
defined as 'viewing all religions as equally valid answers
to the human predicament'.[15] Not dealt with in this book
is *religious inclusivism*, a view held by an increasing
number of Christians who acknowledge Christ as sole

Saviour, but who contend that the sincere Hindu, or ardent Muslim, or faithful adherent of any faith, is saved through Christ without realizing it, much as the God-fearer Cornelius in Acts allegedly was saved before he heard of Christ.[16]

Postmodernists coexist comfortably with religious pluralists but find the proselytizing of religious exclusivists distasteful. Ironically, on university campuses like Cambridge and California, we find intolerance particularly virulent toward open Christian expression of faith in a setting where intellectual freedom of thought is lionized. In assessing the intolerance of politically correct thinking anchored in postmodernism toward the perceived 'intolerance' of religious exclusivism, Carson aptly notes that 'one cannot fail to observe a crushing irony: the gospel of relativistic tolerance is perhaps the most "evangelistic" movement in Western culture at the moment, demanding assent and brooking no rivals.'[17] Open-mindedness has come to be connected not with rational discourse, with listening intently to another's viewpoint, but with an *a priori* commitment to the perspective that holding any viewpoint to be wrong is to be narrow-minded and innately in error. In a gentle but reasoned way, the church must help those gripped in the morass of relativism to understand the syllogism that 'the truth is that there is no truth' is self-refuting and arbitrary, for this statement in itself cannot be true if there is no such thing as truth.[18] The ultimate result of this non self-critiquing relativism is captured in a statement attributed to G.K. Chesterton: 'The problem is that when people stop believing in God, they start to believe in anything.'[19]

The attractiveness of religious pluralism forms a synergy with, or feeds off, excessive individualism, in that it panders to the selective, personalized nature of consumerism, as Netland astutely fingers, 'The availability of many alternative options tends to trivialize and relativize the significance of any one tradition … Pluralization also encourages a consumer mentality regarding religion, which is reflected in a highly pragmatic view of religion, emphasizing what religion does for individuals or society at large and minimizing questions of truth … Related to this is the privatization of religious belief. Religious belief is reduced to a matter of personal taste or expression of personal preference.'[20]

Andy, who along with Dag and Claire are the anti-heroes of the novel, *Generation X*, and whose life ambition seems to be to hang out together, at one point we find getting ready to celebrate Christmas. Andy muses that 'I am buying massive quantities of candles today, but I'm not saying why. Votive candles, birthday candles, emergency candles, dinner candles, Jewish candles, Christmas candles, and candles from the Hindu bookstore bearing peoploid cartoons of saints. They all count – all flames are equal.'[21] Here, then, is a typical postmodern levelling of all religious meanings and events into a universalized blob.

With faith being taken out of the public square, 'live and let live' becomes the religious mantra of the masses. Hence, 'postmoderns are neither antagonistic towards nor strongly interested in a belief system different from their own; they are simply glad that the belief system seems to 'work' for other people.'[22]

Spirituality is cool

Polls reveal that 50 per cent of Canadians believe they have experienced an event before it happened (precognition) and 40 per cent claim to have had some contact with the spirit world.[23] People are fascinated by the paranormal and TV's *Unsolved Mysteries*, no longer giving sole credence to the visible, quantifiable world of the five senses (the scientific worldview). However, they are abandoning traditional sources of where to look for that Higher Power, exchanging Christianity for crystals, yoga, pyramids, and pantheistic ecological or feminist philosophies, largely subsumed under the catch-all title of the New Age Movement. One only has to look in the nearest W.H. Smith bookshop to see that the religious section is crowded with New Age self-help manuals and exotic teachings with little room left on the shelves for 'Christianity'. Shockingly, Colson cites a Gallup poll finding that 20 per cent of Christians in the States believe in reincarnation and 26 per cent in astrology.[24] Even Christians are proving susceptible to New Age spirituality.

The upside to this quest for spiritual meaning is that it is far more possible on the streets of Paris or London to talk about spiritual experiences than it was two decades ago.[25] Summarizing this attitudinal change, Murray remarks that 'postmodernism enhances the process of de-secularization: it endorses the resurgence of spirituality, reflects loss of confidence in rationalism and science and urges pursuit of authentic humanity.'[26] Those who work with Muslims know how easy it is to engage in conversation about God and faith matters with them; the naturalness of doing so is being restored through the postmodern mentality to our western world Generation Xers and Yers in particular.[27] In such an environment, the church has a golden opportunity to counter the current notion that 'democracy shall make you free' with the biblical notion that 'the truth shall make you free'.

But it is an opportunity fraught with difficulty, and only the power of the Holy Spirit and the potency of a living faith can counter the scepticism and irrationality of the current culture. You have to remind yourself that at least a dialogue has opened; otherwise it can be dismaying and intimidating to encounter the postmodern mindset represented by this analysis.

> Now under the influence of Eastern mysticism, many people today would deny that systematic consistency is a test for truth. They affirm that reality is ultimately illogical or that logical contradictions correspond to reality. They assert that in Eastern thought the Absolute or God or the Real transcends the logical categories of human thought. They are apt to interpret the demand for logical consistency as a piece of Western imperialism.[28]

The extreme sport of individualism

In postmodern society, individualism has gone to extremes. So, for instance, the cutting edge of sport seems to have gone beyond the team concept to the dare devil, individualized extremism epitomized by bungee jumping or free fall parachuting, somewhat individualized activities. I might add, Tiplady in *World of Difference*, makes the fascinating point that this trait of postmodernity of individualism can be perceived as culturally dominating by virtue of the fact that mass production technologies have actually resulted in proliferation of choice, not reduction, for now mass customization holds sway.[29]

As a dedicated runner, this means, for example, that I can get my jogging shoes for an aging body customized at www.nike.com/europe to take into account my tendency to lean on my heels, be a size 9½, do 25 miles per week spaced over three runs, and travel along grassy terrain, while not worrying about having the latest bells and whistles on the shoes (not being concerned about making a Nike fashion statement). One report has it that each week in America over two hundred new grocery items enter the marketplace and each year three hundred new magazines are published.[30] We live in a world where proliferation of choice has won out over the economies of scale that mass production promises. To that we owe the wizardry of computerization ... and the postmodern mindset.

While the marvels of modern science and globalization have made extreme individuality possible and popular, they have also conspired to break up the sense of togetherness in family. Rather than playing games, or baking cakes, or having a family devotional time after supper, or debating a topic around the kitchen table at meal time – all regular features of my years growing up in which the TV was absent from our home except during holiday seasons, when one was rented, or borrowed from an aunt – the TV, Walkman, and video games have shrunk families: they may share the same space, but they live in relatively isolated, individualized worlds, where the sense of community has vanished. Intimacy thus is sought vicariously and immorally, whether that is through frankness about private matters on TV talk shows or the simulation of sex in internet chat rooms.[31]

Into such a world lacking intimacy and where loneliness is endemic, the church has something prophetic and counter-cultural to offer. Almost above everything else, the church stands for community, for authentic relationships, and therefore potentially has a powerful basis for reaching out to the postmodern generation. More about that in a coming chapter.

Philosophically, if Self is the centre of Reality and that Reality is largely *constructed* by the environmental influences (conditioning) that one has limited control over, at least in formative years, Reality has no independent existence. What matters then is that one has freedom to make choices, not what the choices are.[32]

Paradoxically, as aptly described by Guder, 'The introduction of media options such as cable and satellite television, as well as video rentals, contributes to fewer and fewer people sharing common experiences, even as they encounter similar images, icons, and story lines.'[33]

If the truth were known, we have become addicted to change and choice. This poses a dilemma for the church because increasingly the unchurched and the younger generation of believers are approaching church involvement with a consumer mentality. People tend to float from church to church, getting a blessing in worship from one church, access to young working adults in a second, and cell (home) group experience in a third. This trend has been well-addressed in *Liquid Church*. Commenting on this tendency in the postmodern church, Carson says, 'Individualism has made an impact on the way religion is conceived. The spread of privatized spirituality, developed apart from a disciplined and disciplining church, doubtlessly fosters desires for personal connection with the transcendent, but, at risk of oxymoron, it is a personally defined transcendence. Privatized spirituality is not conspicuously able to foster care for others.'[34] We will address our response as church in postmodern society in a later chapter as well as see how some growing churches are keeping in step with the Spirit as they keep in touch with culture.

The idolizing of feelings and experience

How stunned I was to read the disturbing book by Neil Postman, *Amusing Ourselves to Death*, a few years ago.

It exposed how extensive was the dumbing down of the American mind (should we rephrase it the western world mind?) in the prioritizing of feeling over thought. No doubt the civilization produced by the Renaissance, the Reformation, and the Enlightenment has elevated reason out of proportion to experience. But one has to be alarmed at the role of television and the computer (e.g. video games) in creating a generation that measures reality in terms of the feelings stimulated by visual images.[35] 'If it feels right, it is moral' is the mantra that dominates decision making in postmodern society. The TV programme, *Sex and the City*, with its emotive power, is likely to influence the ethical values of our generation more than the timeless, propositionally posited Ten Commandments. The upshot of this shift in worldview formation, even for the church, is described fittingly by Dawn.

> The loss of exposition [logical and coherent development of a thesis] must be a major concern for the Church, which tries to pass on faith to the next generation, teach creeds, set out the eminent reasonability of faith, and ground children in doctrines that will duly establish them for growth to maturity in truth and hope. Without theological foundation, faith becomes subject to capricious feelings and to life's troubles.[36]

When push comes to shove, living on the basis of subjective feelings is destructive of character, for it leads away from the objective historicity of our faith to designer faith. It creates a culture needing to be entertained rather than willing to learn cognitively as more stock is put in impressions than in thinking linearly.[37] It creates a generation that no longer perceives emotions to be subject to larger values – like loyalty, honour, duty, social responsibility.[38] As one social commentator observes, 'Postmodernity ... stresses appearance and image over technical and substance; the unique rather than the general; the unrepeatable rather than the reoccurring; the indeterminacy rather than determinism; diversity rather than unity; difference rather than synthesis. It is interested in the eccentric, the marginal, the disqualified, and the subjugated.'[39]

Further exacerbating this ennui over what is right and what is wrong, or over what is of value or what is trash, is the glut of information flowing to us down the world wide web superhighway and various other media so that people do not even have the time to discern what is worth viewing or reading: the search for wisdom has now become information management.

An InterVarsity group in the US drew up a useful taxonomy of the shift from modern to postmodern culture:

- from objective to subjective;
- from autonomous individual to community;
- from the metanarrative to micronarratives;
- from word to image.[40]

In summary, the brave new world is a slave to impressions. MTV sound bites rule. In such a digital universe, rapidly changing scenes overshadow the words within the music; it is really the sound and visual impressions that dominate and speak to most of the five senses head-on. The intellect has given way to sensation. MTV simply symbolizes a paradigm shift whereby postmodern society determines reality or truth to a large extent on the basis of feeling and image, not reason or logic.

Pragmatism overshadows altruism

Related to the above is the push to measure value and truth in terms of 'does it work?' Anthropologist Paul Hiebert explains this philosophical shift succinctly: 'If we cannot test for truth, on what basis can we judge between scientific theories? The answer is pragmatism – the "useful fictions" that are good if they are useful and if they work. The purpose of science, therefore, is not to find truth about the external world but to control it for our own purposes.'[41]

Somewhat a function of technology, this utilitarianism even drives the postmodern search for spiritual meaning. It is a search that is 'highly subjective [with] everything directed to the self; one's ego determines the value of everything'.[42]

The upside of this drift toward pragmatism is that Generation X and Y youth insist on a Christianity that works; the separation of faith and action is not tolerated (Jas. 1:27; 2:14–26). Along the same lines, the cry for mentoring is a plea for authenticity in faith issues – surely to be applauded.

Conclusion

This chapter would end nicely with an exposition of how the borderless church could respond constructively and contextually to postmodernity in the western world. However, that forms the heart of the book, along with a strategy for counteracting religious pluralism, so it begs special attention in its own chapter, which it shall have in Chapter 5. The appetizer we can offer you now is that the missional church of the future must emphasize relational community, a holistic approach to ministry, genuine worship, and applied (practical) teaching of the Word, all within the context of reaching out in mission.

Joel Dylhoff, a Christian, speaks for his generation, most wired by postmodernity, and offers hope: 'My generation, it is said, has dropped out. This is not true. We're here on the sidelines, looking for ways to get involved. We need a sense of direction to channel our efforts. By working together with the older generations, Generation X is poised to make its contribution to society. Anyone want to help?'[43]

4. How the West Was Won

How ironic that in an age jettisoning the past, the church in the west is poised on the edge of a precipice. The consequences will be disastrous if she fails to heed lessons of history that can offer a way of escape from the church's growing ineffectiveness. An obstacle can be turned into an opportunity if lessons from the past are heeded. In a world increasingly hostile to any message claiming a monopoly on truth, today's church would do well to learn from the church of the first several centuries, which faced similar cultural conditions and yet flourished beyond all expectations. Within three centuries, what had started as a motley crew of 12 unsophisticated disciples spawned a movement of 10 million believers in a Roman Empire numbering 50 million people.[1] Let us look, then, at parallels between their world and ours, ascertaining how we can apply their dynamic for growth to our own situation.

Uncanny resemblance

1 Globalization

Not without reason, the Scripture refers to Christ being born at precisely the right time: 'But when *the time had fully come*, God sent his Son, born of a woman ...' (Gal. 4:4, italics added). As Green puts it, 'the new faith entered the world at a time of peace unheralded in history. The whole known world was for the first time under the effective grip of one power – Rome.'[2] Indeed a road system linked far-flung corners of the Roman Empire. An inscription found at Hierapolis on the tomb of a merchant indicates that he travelled to Rome 72 times during the era of the NT, a previously unheard of frequency of travel (one immediately thinks by comparison of the transatlantic speed of the Boeing 747 and the instant communication of the Internet in the current age).[3] Furthermore, there was a common language linking diverse peoples of the Empire – Greek – just as today English is the language of commerce, computer, and entertainment across the globe, even if it is not the native language of most of the world's population (think of the fact that the NT was written in street Greek even though Jesus and his disciples were native Aramaic or Hebrew-speaking people). To cap it all, the universal cultural influence was Greek philosophy and values: today it is the globalizing influence of western culture which creates a universalizing and digitalized tsunami through MTV, Hollywood movies, McDonalds-type Trans National Corporations, and Microsoft-friendly technologies.

2 Religious pluralism

In much the same way that the current scorn in the belief in One Way smothers monotheistic witness, the early church faced scepticism by a Greek-dominated worldview that denied that deity could be embodied in one being (1 Cor. 1 and 2).[4] Scriptural passages like Revelation 2 and 3 reveal that the early church constantly wrestled with influences of a diversity of religions and cults.[5] Nor let us forget that on Mars Hill, Paul was overwhelmed by a plethora of deities (Acts 17).

What we call atheism today had a completely different connotation in the times of Jesus and Paul. Christians did not honour the customary deities and were therefore labelled atheists. *Religio*, or the state religion, was distinguished from *superstitio*, or private faith, the latter being tolerated if the former was acknowledged.[6] Making the rejection of the practice of *religio* by Christians hazardous to their health, even if inevitable because of their convictions (Acts 4:12, 19–20), was the deifying of the emperor. In the words of the ancient poet Virgil with reference to emperor worship, 'This is the man; this is the one whom you have long been promised, Augustus Caesar, offspring of a god, founder of a golden age'.[7] Augustus Caesar simply revived the state cult that had been falling into disuse even as the Empire was slipping into decline. Caesar's successor, Tiberius, ruled during the life of Christ and continued the tradition of accepting worship. It was not really until emperors later in the century – namely, Nero and Domitian, prominent in the life of Paul and John – however, that we find virulent persecution of Christians breaking out. It would be Christians' unwillingness to separate their public from private lives that marked them out for suffering, and even martyrdom, as in their savage torturing in Nero's gardens in AD 64.

Paradoxically, then, while religious diversity was encouraged, it came at the expense of compromising the exclusive claims of Christian faith. A Christian would rather die than participate in public festivals acknowledging Caesar's deity even though allowed to worship according to conscience in private. As Kostenberger contends, 'Overall, it appears that the greatest problem faced by believers at the time Revelation was written was not the question of how to dialogue with adherents of other faiths, but rather the issue of how to keep their Christian practice clean from associations with their pagan environment.'[8] Thus, religious pluralism and a contradictory definition of religious tolerance held sway in much the same way as the 'thought police' do today. We navigate our way carefully so as to maintain the integrity of our convictions about Christ while respecting the beliefs of others (cf. 1 Pet. 2:11).

3 Search for belonging

Increasingly, in the days when the early church was establishing a foothold in the Roman Empire, the social needs of the individual were no longer being fully met in the city state or household and so volunteer associations (*collegia*) or guilds proliferated. This created a sense of community and status for individuals that set them apart from others.[9] Not surprisingly, the state tended to think of Christianity as being yet another form of voluntary association, in other words, harmless, because culturally friendly.[10] The church was perceived progressively as a caring, socially-conscious community – much as this loving inclusiveness, where it is found today in the church, attracts postmodern people cut adrift socially and emotionally because of the dysfunctionality of family backgrounds. Imagine the social implications of Paul urging Philemon to accept back his escaped slave, Onesimus, on an equal footing, as a brother in the Lord. People were forming new social alliances, and the church was perceived as an attractive alternative for the oppressed, the poor, and the marginalized. Often quoted for his insight into the lay quality of Christian witness in contrast to that of clergy, the second century pagan, Celcius, stated that it was the 'wool-workers, cobblers, laundry-workers and the most illiterate and bucolic yokels' who spread the gospel.[11] Essentially, though, it was the Holy Spirit pouring the love of God into hearts of new converts (Rom. 5:5) that enabled them to treat one another as brothers and sisters in Christ: a *koinonia* or 'fellowship' (Acts 2:42–5) drew most unlikely companions into an intimate community that offered something remarkable. It is not uncommon to hear it posited that the extraordinary growth of the early church was due primarily to the revolutionary sense of community 'which was open to all but required absolute and exclusive loyalty and involved every aspect of a believer's life'.[12]

4 Inclusiveness

Relatedly, there was a breaking down of traditional social strata, with a new spirit of inclusiveness fomenting change, much as we see in the recalibrating of social values today. A decade ago it would have been unheard of in the western world for gays living together to be granted the same marital status as heterosexuals. Racism and religious intolerance would have been endemic in society less than a generation ago, whereas inclusivism on all levels reigns today (at least on paper). By comparison, in NT times, freedmen (former slaves) had achieved high social advancement (e.g. Felix in Acts 23:24).[13] The church was even more iconoclastic in her inclusiveness, declaring that in Christ race, gender and economic status were not a basis for discrimination (Gal. 3:28; Eph. 2:11ff.). How the outside world must have marvelled when they witnessed the new respect given to women (e.g. eight of the twenty-six Christians greeted in Romans 16 by Paul were women). Further proof of the liberating power of the gospel was the inclusion of the many in the advance of that same gospel: ministry was not the privy of the super-apostles but of teams of multi-gifted people. Sometimes we miss this element to the church being planted around the Mediterranean world, as was the case with the team ministry of Paul, Silvanus, and Timothy, for instance, as described in 1 Thessalonians.

5 Loose morals

Rampant sexual immorality in the Roman Empire escalating even as the state slid into decline is well-documented. It is symbolized by the dissolute lifestyle of Caligula as ruler (also known as Gaius, assassinated in AD 41). The antics of the imperial cult became something of a soap opera, not unlike the behaviour we have come to associate with certain leaders of the western world. Commenting on this moral deterioration in the Roman Empire at the time of Christ, Green says, 'It has been well said of the Greeks that it was not that men became so depraved that they abandoned their gods, but rather that the gods became so depraved that they were abandoned by men.'[14]

Today, we observe a correlation between declining moral standards in society at large and slippage into a post-Christian society – whether that be related to the explosion of premarital and extramarital sex, the proliferation of pornography, the breakdown of marriage, the escalation of crimes of violence, or the self-serving corruption of company executives. Meanwhile, the church that is vilified as being redundant and self-righteous becomes at the same time a magnet for those disillusioned with promiscuity and a lack of centeredness. Ironically, early Christians were vilified as immoral and accused by far-fetched tales of cannibalism and incest. Even as today the language of Christians can be misunderstood and misrepresented, so the emerging first- to third-century church had to contend with mischievous interpretations shaped by the fact that congregations met in secret, used expressions about feeding on Christ, and spoke of loving those whom they called brothers and sisters.[15] Like them, our proclaimed high standards of morality are both our strength and our source of vulnerability. Early Christians did not attend gladiatorial games; today we have various convictions and practices of separation from the world, inviting ridicule as the church is fingered for 'being so heavenly minded that we are of no earthly good'. Early Christians would not become soldiers; while not uniformly upheld, some contemporary Christians are known for their pacifism.[16]

6 Marginality of the church

Anything new tends to be at the margins of society, so we should not be surprised by the knowledge that the Christian faith did not dominate the then known world just because its founder had risen from the dead and the book of Acts refers to Christians as 'turning the world upside down'. Uncertain as to how to classify these religious upstarts, the Romans referred to Christians somewhat derogatorily as 'the third race'.[17] In a third category after Romans and Jews, Christians felt ill at ease with this epithet, especially as they sought to win a hearing from their pagan friends.[18] See the uncanny resemblance to our day and age? The church today in the western world is viewed as an anachronism by the power brokers of society: Christianity is considered as being made up of anti-intellectuals and nobodies. This is not a caricature the church lives with comfortably.

Not until the fall of Rome in AD 410 did church leadership (the bishop of Rome) seek to move centre stage politically, justifying his management of the material aspects of society in Italy. A movement intent on winning the lost gradually degenerated into an institution motivated by self-preservation.

The Thessalonian church: missional church model

Putting a face on missionality theory is one of the purposes of writing this book. How then to make the early church come alive as we seek to demonstrate that the church exists for mission, that God's intent for the church is that she should not be thought of as a building, that her missional DNA makes her morph without borders? One only need turn to the NT to unearth a missional church treasure – in Thessalonica.

Most data about this church is found in 1 and 2 Thessalonians and Acts 17. Thessalonica was the capital city of Macedonia on the important Egnatia Way, the motorway from the hinterlands to Rome (modern day Salonika in Greece stands on its site). Paul probably wrote 1 Thessalonians in AD 50 while he was at Corinth; 2 Thessalonians was probably written only a few months later, making this correspondence the second earliest Pauline letter after Galatians. Astoundingly, Paul had planted what turned out to be a flourishing church in the short space of three weeks, according to Acts 17:1–15.

What is germane to our explication of missional church, though, is what we learn about this church, especially in 1 Thessalonians 1. There we discover three hallmarks of a healthy church in a world similar to ours today:
1. She provided a community where faith was lived out authentically.

2. She made a missional impact on her immediate surroundings.
3. She not only had a local testimony but a global reach.

A community with authentic faith

Repeatedly in the early verses of the book, the apostle Paul speaks highly of the change in character of those who had only recently worshipped idols: 'you became a model to all the believers in Macedonia and Achaia' (v. 7; cf. 3:6). Paul's prayers for them are filled with gratitude for their 'work produced by faith ... labour prompted by love, and ... endurance inspired by hope' (v. 3; cf. 2:20). Paul could speak of them as being 'imitators of us' (v. 6). Apparently they did not fall away in the face of persecution but went from strength to strength (v. 6; cf. 2:14). The Thessalonians were into spiritual formation. So often, churches with a strong missional emphasis are perceived as focusing obsessively on 'doing' rather than 'being'. The Thessalonian church, evidently, balanced her *evangelism* with her *edification* ministry. That radiant faith must have been in itself a great drawing card to the pagan masses. Discerning this Christ-illuminating quality of missional churches intrinsically, Guder observes

> Key images of God's alternative community, the missional church, are found in the Gospels' description of the people of God as 'the salt of the earth', and a 'city set on a hill'. These images suggest that mission is not just what the church *does*; it is what the church *is*. Saltiness is not an action; it is the very character of salt. Similarly, light or a city on a hill need not do anything in order to be seen. So too it is with God's 'sent people'.[19]

One might say that the church was missional by 'being' *and* by intentional witness. That 'being' included demonstrating the love of Christ practically – by spontaneously providing for the poor, tending to the sick, caring for widows and orphans, and going into homes to cast out evil spirits and heal the sick (cf. 1 Tim. 5:3–15; 1 Cor. 16:1–3; Jas. 5:14–15).[20] One cannot read the NT without giving credence to 'power evangelism' subsequent to the life of Christ in the gospels; in 1 Thessalonians 1, Paul refers to the first converts as receiving the Word 'with power, with the Holy Spirit and with deep conviction' (v. 5). Commenting on the nature of this 'being' of the early church and her evangelistic drawing power, church historian Harnack observes: 'The new language on the lips of Christians was the language of love. But it was more than a language; it was a thing of power and action.'[21]

Christians remained in Alexandria during the bubonic plague of AD 256 to succour the sick and dying while the rest of the population fled. Our terms 'hospital' and 'hospice' derive from 'hospitality', not unexpectedly, given the long-established practice from early centuries of the church harbouring the outcasts of society, such as lepers.[22] Often this practical expression of love was first found within the church community, as we see in the book of Acts, where believers pooled possessions so that the needy had their material necessities met (4:32–5).

Intentionality of witness has been picked up on more acutely by the modern missionary movement, marshalling support for its approach to world evangelization. In the Thessalonian church, as in other early churches, this would almost certainly have included following Paul's example in the sending out of itinerant missionaries (or apostles). Unlike bishops, elders, and deacons, such missionaries were roving.[23] But the everyday form of witness by lay people in the blacksmith shop, on the farm, and in the neighbourhood would have been crucial to spreading the Word through the local church. The exhortation of Paul in his second letter to the church in which he stresses the importance of work to witness (3:7–9) indicates that early on in the discipling process it was taught and modelled that mission was not disconnected from everyday life or a matter of special calling, but encompassed everyone's local as well as some people's global witness. It therefore required a lifestyle where walk and talk were blended seamlessly. The modern separation of life into sacred and secular spheres was not a pathology found in early church life. In actual fact, although there were missionaries, as Murray provocatively argues, 'We know of few "missionaries" in pre-Christendom ... Evangelism was a lifestyle, not a specialist activity. The Christendom shift fractured this integration of church and mission.'[24]

A community blossoming where planted

Her church planter could have stopped singing the Thessalonians' praises there. What Paul had already described was an exemplary church. But Paul goes on to laud the Thessalonians because 'the Lord's message rang out from you ... in Macedonia and Achaia [in their neighbourhood and environs]' (1 Thes. 1:8). The word translated as 'rang out' is the same one used to describe the trumpet call heralding the arrival of a dignitary or royalty, and that it is found here in the perfect tense suggests that the witness was no passing whim.[25] There was evidently purpose in the witness of these early Christians, characteristic of churches of the first few centuries generally. They were not overwhelmed by their marginal status in society, nor did they shy away from defending the faith in the face of religious pluralism, nor did they keep quiet because of the risk of persecution. Although situated in an urban setting, at a crossroads in the Empire, these former pagans had not been afraid to 'turn from idols ... to serve a living and true God' (v. 9). They had heeded the last words of Christ, found in Acts 1:8, to be witnesses in their equivalent of Jerusalem and Samaria, and to the culturally identical and near unreached, that is, in Macedonia and Achaia. Evidently this church moved smoothly between 'inreach' and 'outreach'. They were borderless – in the sense that all that mattered did not occur in their house church gatherings alone but in the neighbourhood, too.

A community with a world vision

Not content with local or nearby mission, the Thessalonian church intentionally reached out to the larger Mediterranean world. Thus Paul raves: 'The Lord's message rang out from you, *not only* in Macedonia and Achaia – your faith in God has become known everywhere' (v. 8, italics added). The 'everywhere' went beyond Macedonia and Achaia, the Thessalonians' immediate urban and provincial locality. One has to conclude that the Thessalonian mission was far-reaching. Even the verb used to describe this witness, 'become known', is descriptive of directional and aggressive action. Therefore, it would not be far-fetched to see this church as one which had carefully followed the full teaching of Acts 1:8. Along with reaching her Jerusalem and Judea, she had sought to proclaim the good news 'unto the uttermost parts of the earth'. Mission was a both/and proposition, not an either/or one whereby witness locally was pitted against global mission. Churches today with the both/and mentality are being labelled *glocal* churches. That glocal understanding is essential to being borderless as a church – and the Thessalonian church was just that.

Points to ponder about the past

In this chapter we have given a brief survey of how the early church grew in circumstances similar to our own as we enter the twenty-first century. How points from Rome westward were won (Rom. 15:18–33) in the first several centuries of church history inform our own postmodern, globalized, and pluralistic world. At the end of the day, the early church was missional and that's what gave her the Spirit-infused impetus to rise to the occasion. She was a borderless church, not only because for the first one hundred and fifty years she did not meet in church buildings,[26] but because she had the 20:20 vision (see Acts 20:20) of gossiping the good news everywhere – around the corner and around the world.

5. Soft Apologetics: Declaring the Uniqueness of Christ in a Postmodern and Religiously Plural World

In electioneering leading up to the 2004 Canadian federal election, the Prime Minister, Paul Martin, quietly polled Ontarians asking if they were 'more or less likely to vote for the Conservative/Alliance if you knew they had been taken over by evangelical Christians'.[1] The leader of the Conservative/Alliance party, Stephen Harper, was characterized as 'radical and right wing' and 'very non-mainstream' with a 'very American style'. Implied in this poll was a kind of conspiracy theory that reminded one of anti-Semitism. Evangelicals were painted as a fringe group to be afraid of – even though 12 per cent of the population were Protestant evangelicals and another seven per cent Roman Catholics who shared the same fundamental beliefs. This perspective is symptomatic of a postmodern culture that is tolerant, but in a selective way, with mainstream Christianity having to fight for fair press. About the growing hostility toward the religious exclusivism that Christianity represents, Carson has this cogent statement to make.

> Open-mindedness ... no longer means that you may or may not have strong views yet remain committed to listening honestly to countervailing arguments. Rather, it means that you are dogmatically committed to the view that all

convictions that any view whatsoever is wrong are improper and narrow-minded. In other words, open-mindedness has come to be identified with not the means of rational discourse, but with certain conclusions. The irony is that Christians are a barely tolerated minority on most university campuses.[2]

In chapters 2 and 3 we did a biopsy of the western world with respect to its essentially postmodern and religiously plural makeup. When a hooker sells her 2-year-old daughter to paedophiles so that she can maintain her drug habit, and in desperately seeking for help is asked if she has thought of turning to the church, to which she reacts with horror and disbelief, such stories should cause us to rethink how we are convincing a sceptical world of the claims of Christ. The message (wine) is unchanging, but the methods (wineskins) need replacing. For instance, while the Bible consistently rejects other religions as being salvific, see the Ten Commandments (Deut. 5:7–9), and elsewhere, sometimes even in harsh language (e.g. Is. 37:18–19; Jer. 2:11–13; Jn. 3:36; Rom. 1:18–25), do we really need to harangue unbelievers? Just as a soft landing on Mars makes all the difference to the success of a space probe, so a gentle, in the sense of contextualized and relational, defence of the gospel, is the tonic for a 'leave me alone' yet searching world.

Soft-landing gospel

So how can we land the space probe on cratered, rocky terrain? Here are a half dozen key components that have already been alluded to in examining the early church's development and which will surface again as we look at contemporary missional churches. They are biblical components and they are contextual, that is, suited to the environment, the mission field in which churches find themselves. The components needed in the space craft to allow for a soft landing are a community of belonging, worship that is God-centred and experiential, equipping that allows for profound lay involvement, holistic ministry emphasis, taking and applying the Word of God seriously, relational and knowledgeable but non-confrontational witness, and balancing local with global witness.

Churches where there is a sense of belonging

It is instructive to see the growth of the house and cell church movement in our day.

Note this informed observation: 'The emerging generation of the under-thirties is rapidly moving back from a post-Christendom to a pre-Christian culture. Among them classic cell church is working well.'[3] Driven by dysfunctionality in the home and cynicism about the ulterior motives of corporations and government, younger postmoderns tune out those with whom they have not formed a close relationship and in whom they have not learned to trust.[4] Small groups or tribes work for them. On the other side of the world, take China for instance, where it is estimated that twenty thousand people daily become believers, most of those added to the church through house groups. If non-western people, let alone postmodern people who are predominately in the western world, focus on building community and relationships to the exclusion of individualism and institutional loyalty, we should not be surprised that missional churches will understand the power of the small group to reach the lost by satisfying that need for belonging. The small group my wife and I are part of includes those with special needs for belonging: single mothers, divorcees, a new young adult believer from an unchurched family, and a registered-as-blind widower.

In one sense, one can argue that the success of the Alpha Course, beginning with five courses in the UK in 1992, and as late as 1998 proliferating to 10,500, is in part attributable to conversation about faith issues over food, repeated week after week, as relationships form. The renowned Willow Creek Community Church, with over twenty thousand people gathered weekly, is driven in her success as much by her 2700 small groups as she is by being seeker-friendly, including through the communication skills of lead pastor Bill Hybels. Callahan is on target in declaring that 'people come to a church in our time with a search for community, not committee ... They are looking for home, for relationships.'[5]

Even mega-churches keep growing because they have discovered the evangelistic potency of small groups. We shall see this truth as we explore Mars Hill Church with its ten thousand attendees – a church that did not exist seven years ago. In spite of what we will contend shortly about worship as being a linchpin of missional churches, the fact remains that in North America (only slightly different statistics in Europe) surveys indicate that 95 per cent of unbelievers are converted through friends, not style of worship or evangelistic programmes.[6]

Communal approaches to learning are personal and thus connect with postmoderns suspicious of too much emphasis on reason.[7] For example, God's love is revealed as seekers or those invited by friends share a common meal with 'insiders' so that weeks later, as they hear 1 Corinthians 13 read in a service, the love truth hits home. Interestingly, the word *companionship* comes from the Latin *cum* + *panis* loosely translated as *breading together* – not far from the evangelical joke that we ought to rename church *fellowship* as *foodship*.[8]

Adding synergy to this communal dynamic is the potential of small groups and cell churches to harness the spiritual gifts found in the Body. Releasing those gifts through early use, there being no large assembly of believers to fade anonymously into, missional momentum occurs. Miley captures this as he expresses a longing to see mission rooted in community, not distant programmes.

> Community is the environment of extended family. It is committed relationships developed over time in the midst of real life, providing nurture, support, accountability, and staying power for the long haul. Most believers will not leave home and move somewhere else to participate in a mission. … If their unique contribution to God's global purpose is to be made, it will take place right where they are, in the context of Christian community of which they are a part – their church. Church is not a series of religious meetings. It is a way of life.[9]

Worship is missional when it works

During my eight years of pastoring in two churches, worship wars were an undercurrent of our church life. Not as bad as what I heard when comparing notes with some other pastors, but as predictable as freckles on a redhead's face, nonetheless. Notwithstanding the knack of worship disputes to sabotage the kingdom single-mindedness of churches, corporate worship needs to work and not be downplayed in missional churches. While worship is not limited to our singing, music is such a dominant factor in our culture that church worship is borderless. That is, it is not only for believers present, but for a fascinated world 'feeling and believing'. Crossover musical bands like Delirious verify global fascination with Christian music.

When God is genuinely the subject of our worship, that acknowledging of his *weorth* (Old English for *honour*) and *scipe* (signifying *to create*)[10] has tremendous evangelistic clout. 'God inhabits the praises of his people', Scripture declares (Ps. 22:3, AV). Observing this connection between worship (which technically can only be engaged in and truly experienced by believers) and witness, Ward exhorts: 'If we want to learn how to fish, we need to truly believe that people want God. The fish rises to the bait; they are feeding. So liquid church would reshape itself around worshipers as consumers [those shopping for God].'[11]

When I participated in worship services in rural India in my years as a missionary, it was not uncommon for Hindu villagers to peer into the pane-less windows or hang around the edges of the tent in the field to listen to the singing and the message. That's how worship in borderless churches should be – for the saints inside and for the sinners outside. The one group connects with God when focused on him and the other does so vicariously. Worship may trigger the start of a spiritual odyssey that leads to Christ for the gothic pagan just as the rich community life may woo the second generation British Muslim. Muslims are regularly drawn to consider the Saviour as a result of listening to Christians pray. Sufism within Islam is a crying out to know God experientially. Worship that is theocentric and not anthropocentric is not a matter of the medium (traditional versus contemporary, for example) but whether worshippers are really trying to bring delight to the one God who alone is worthy. For that commitment we do not have to apologize to onlookers, for they also are searching for that Source that lifts them outside of their miserable selves. Again, it is not a matter of creating the right feeling or orchestrating the right mood, but of the purpose of the worship. Styles are secondary.

That said, in my view, the most powerful form of worship involves content that focuses on God's attributes, or what he has done for us, *and* musical styles with which people are familiar. Hymns don't have to have all the content nor are contemporary modes necessarily popular with everyone. I like what Dawn says about worship in this regard: 'Genuine praise of God involves all our emotions and needs, not by focusing on ourselves, but by proclaiming God's truth and God's actions and attributes on our behalf ... Only when we see God as he truly is can we know ourselves aright – and then we can respond with offerings of praise.'[12]

Somehow mega-churches have grasped the missional value of worship. Their seeker-friendly services have found ways to include non-believers in the act of the corporate worship of God's people. Unabashedly, Rick Warren, founder and senior pastor of Saddleback Church in the US, with its twenty-five thousand members, links the two when he says: 'The Bible tells us that "the Father seeks [worshipers]" (John 4:23) so evangelism is the task of recruiting worshipers of God.'[13]

Come what may, there is an increasing convergence among churches of all persuasions and traditions that are combining style and substance in worship that augers well for the borderless church of the future, looking for models in how to do it. Daniel Harrell, who has led innovative attempts to attract young adults at historic Park Street Church in Boston, Massachusetts, addresses this trend perceptively in these words

> Unlike previous worship reforms that generally stressed authenticity in terms of spoken words conforming to truth

(grounded in Scripture), the focus now is on authenticity of religious experience: 'it's got to *feel* real.'

This should not be construed as merely an episode of positive, subjective feelings, but as an unmistakeable engagement with the numinous – the self-validating presence of God in the midst of his gathered people. This does not replace the primacy of Scripture, but is viewed as an essential companion.[14]

Equipping and empowering the laity

People need a sense of purpose in life. That's the way God created us. When a celebrity-obsessed world looks inside the goldfish bowl of church life, it finds its stereotypes challenged, for here 'everybody is somebody' – instead of the pastor being the resident celebrity. Small groups have the unofficial function of breaking up fallow ground; they fragment and disperse power coalescing around the professional clergy. Being ordained myself and experiencing the temptations that come with being 'Reverend', I applaud efforts to decentralize ministry, as I do in the chapter in my book on servant leadership called 'Impartiality: Not Being Impressed by Power'.[15] In actual fact, the biblical word from which we get the English word *clergy*, *kleros*, connotes *inheritance* or *heir* (1 Pet. 1:4; Gal. 3:29; Col. 1:12; Acts 20:32; 26:18) and thus refers to the whole people of God and not a select few that become full-time clergy.[16] Borderless churches such as Mars Hill, in fact, increasingly avoid using the term, laity, because it immediately creates a sense of distinction in people's minds between those paid for doing ministry (considered more spiritual) and those not paid for doing ministry (considered as amateurs).

Inimical to discipleship is learning by doing. Learning as a passive pew warmer is counterproductive. My 21 years with Operation Mobilization (OM) taught me the Rabbinic style of learning, the method used by Jesus, which allowed followers of great teachers immediately to put into practice the knowledge divulged by their master guru (Mt. 10). There's something about jumping off the deep end of the swimming pool that frees you to learn to swim. It can also lead to drowning, so we do need to be wary of the cavalier attitude displayed when assigning great responsibilities to novices. At any rate, we must remind ourselves that the goal of evangelism is not converts but disciples (Mt. 28:19).

Lest we question this interpretation of the Great Commission in Matthew 28:16–20, the baptizing (v. 19) and the 'teaching them to obey everything I have commanded you' (v. 20) are adverbial participles modifying the main verb, 'make disciples'. Part of discipleship, of course, is learning what your spiritual gifts are and being released into ministry that enables you to exercise those self-same gifts (Eph. 4:12–16). All that to say that discipleship is at the heart of the church's mission; it is just as much related to her *evangelistic* calling as her *edifying* role. As Guder puts it: 'Whereas discipleship was understood by the first- and second-century faith communities as the practice of Christian witness, it became more and more the fulfilment of the ethical, moral, and liturgical requirements that would guarantee entry into heaven.'[17]

Let us remind ourselves of the need to make ancient history current: our review in Chapter 3 of early church history irrefutably demonstrated the power of the laity in effecting church growth. Why should the emphasis be on training and utilizing the laity in church ministry? Well, simply because the NT focus is not on the clergy (not mentioned as distinguished from the laity until Clement in AD 95) but on the *laos*, that is, the whole people of God (1 Pet. 2:9–10).[18] Every intentional and informal attempt to train, to equip, and to mentor the laity will pay dividends in maximizing the potential of the church to reach a lost world for Christ. The NT word for 'equipping', for example, *katartizo*, implies a path to progress that will take some time, and will be labour-intensive.[19]

I am sometimes asked why it is that OM has been so successful in training leaders. My 'best guess' is the way our teams functioned. Everyone on the team had a responsibility. In India, on a team of ten people in 1973, I started out managing the literature – making sure that we had an adequate supply of literature in Hindi, English, Urdu, and a small quantity of books and free literature in six or so other languages. I had to keep literature clean from the dust of the Ganges plains in the summer drought, free of mildew in the monsoons, and clear of white ants that ate it in our storage base. Giving out up to one hundred thousand tracts a week with a highly mobile truck team meant I had to think ahead lest we run out of our mainstay evangelistic material.

Proving myself in that area (never having done anything quite like it before), I graduated to driving the truck. That had been my dream going overland to India in a ten-ton British lorry in 1972, but I was not used to driving a standard, double-clutching, right-hand drive vehicle on the left side of the road! I did not get to take the OM driver's test until I had been in India for six months.

Having avoided running over too many dogs (and definitely no cows), after driving the team truck for some months, I then got thrust temporarily into team leadership. One thing led to another and I got stuck in that role. All that is to say that learning what my spiritual gifts were came by trial and error, by imitating, and by a carefully-monitored team environment. Team work meant everyone was released into ministry. In the same vein, what Stephens articulates in his excellent book on the subject, resonates with me: 'The environment itself must communicate that the whole body together has clerical status.'[20] Not by accident, Rick Warren's church of *Purpose Driven* fame identifies one of her five criteria for being purpose-driven as the equipping of disciples.[21]

Essential to the empowering of the laity is not only taking risks by putting them into ministry earlier rather than later but also by leaders modelling and mentoring. Up-close-and-personal is freeing for the younger Christian who needs to see leaders as normal people – those who make mistakes even while demonstrating self-discipline and other character traits they aspire to emulate. Young people will not take seriously those they are supposed to follow who are inaccessible and unwilling to be vulnerable.[22] Relating this to missionaries, Tiplady observes: 'Whilst modernist Veteran/Boomer missionaries want and expect their leaders to be strong and confident, postmodern Xer missionaries want to see their leaders express an awareness of their own weaknesses and failings.'[23]

Generation X and Y Christians want leaders to be their friends. I was struck by receiving an email from a 27-year-old member of our organization whom I had invited to join a brainstorming group, addressing me as 'friend'. People are longing for the 'give and take' between leader and follower that was demonstrated by Jesus. Pleads another Generation Xer, 'we will listen to the oldest generation give us instruction on principles attentively and respectively ... Credibility and age are intertwined. Generation X wants to hear from the oldest what principles they used to focus and organize their lives.'[24]

Leaders need to allow themselves to be demytholo-
gized. Distance only reinforces the professional versus
amateur distinction between laity and clergy, between
staff and management. Interestingly, *amateur* comes
from a Latin word meaning to do something for love.
Ironically, it is the amateur in church life who often best
models how service should be conducted, out of the joy
of serving the Lord freely, and not as a paid professional
duty.

Holistic ministry

Although there tend to be major differences between
North American and European views on this subject,
Bosch is not far from the mark when he contends that
Luke 4:16–21 has replaced Matthew 28:16–20 as the
pivotal text for understanding Christ's mission and that
of the church.[25]

Let me clarify what I just said about the continental
divide. Increasingly churches on both sides of the
Atlantic – let alone in the majority world – the ones
which would describe themselves as *missional*, converge
around a commitment to holistic ministry. Whether it is
the Thy Kingdom Come Church (Chapter 11) ministering
to drug addicts or the New Life Church (Chapter 8)
with a community-focused vision and involvement
globally with a strong emphasis on ministering to the
whole person, word and deed missions flow seamlessly
together. Church planting ministry, as our own
organization, AWM, is affirming, must address the social
and economic needs of receptor audiences often living
with poverty or various forms of injustice, so that, as we
tackle problems of body, soul, and spirit holistically, the
result is transformational in society, what is sometimes
called *transformational development*.[26]

Mission viewed this way means that when pharma-
ceutical companies spend less than one per cent of their
research and development budgets on major illnesses in
the developing world, an English church cries foul and
addresses the problems presented by the gaunt face of
AIDS victims in sub-Saharan Africa.[27] There is an injustice
that we feel driven to correct when we know that the
richest 225 individuals in the world have a combined
annual income equal to that of the poorest 47 per cent
of the global population and the three richest people on
earth have assets greater than the combined GDP of the
48 least developed nations.[28]

The radicalness of the word

My experience of pastoring convinced me that people do
want serious spiritual feeding. We have been schooled
to believe that the day of expositional preaching is over,
that a visually over-stimulated generation has too short
of an attention span to handle anything but spiritual
junk food.[29] Junk food is instantly gratifying but does not
satisfy in the long run, in fact may lead to malnutrition
if the habit is not kicked. Attendance increased in the
churches I pastored, even though I emphasized feeding
the sheep rather than grazing them. True, such preaching
has to be relevant, applied to everyday life, peppered with
illustrations or stories, and frequently using Power-Point
or a mixture of communication techniques. Combined
with worship that is pregnant with substance *and* style,
preaching that takes content *and* context seriously is
attractive to postmoderns. I echo Dawn's words: 'God's
Word, rightly read and heard, will shake us up. God
cannot bear our sin and wants to put to death our self-
centeredness … Everything that we do in worship should
kill us, but especially the parts of the service in which we

hear the Word.'[30] And that's the radical word that people instinctively want: 'tell us like it is', they say, a sign of the Spirit of God stirring hearts.

'Rightly dividing the word of truth' becomes all the more urgent in an age of blurring the lines between virtual reality and actual reality. We need not be apologetic that in treasuring propositional revelation enshrined in Scripture, we are thumbing our nose at the politically correct notion that there is none of what Francis Schaeffer used to describe in his writings as 'true truth'. The Bible gives a confused world a coherent foundation for ethics and a compass for dealing with the unfamiliar terrain of pluralism.

Like a piece of metal flitting between magnetic poles, postmodern humankind is trapped between conflicting desires for the rationality of modernity and the reality defined by feelings and experience of postmodernity. What Christianity and the word of God can speak into this tension is an admission that claims of objectivity are shaped by context *but* that we who 'see through a glass darkly' can nonetheless have confidence that God in his wisdom has chosen a medium of communication (the Scripture – but not limited to that) that sheds sufficient light on reality, on truth, for us to break out of the murkiness bred by a fallen world.

Furthermore, it is partly the communal dimension of us that requires truth to be grasped collectively, a knowing that reaches beyond the purely rational.[31] The Muslims understand this. They accuse Christians of corrupting the text of our Book. But upon closer examination, Muslims understand corruption of sacred documents to take two forms: one involves an altering of the words in the text – what we might normally think of when considering textual corruption. That is called *tahrif-i lafzi* (Qur'an 2:75 –9). However, upon closer examination, it is corruption of meaning by the way the believing community lives out the meaning of the text that is in view in the Qur'an. This form of corruption is called *tahrif-i ma'nawi* (Qur'an 3:78–9; 4:44–7; 5:12–5), and involves corruption by not practising the Truth and so misleading onlookers (cf. 1 Jn. 3:17–8).[32] Profoundly, Islam has discerned the role of community in arriving at, or at least accurately mirroring, the truth of God's written word. In fact, the significant role of the church in mediating the revelation provided humankind by the Holy Spirit became a dividing wedge between Protestants and Roman Catholics, the latter claiming that the Holy Spirit works through the church (the community of God's people) to provide inspired, infallible truth, while the former body of Christians contended that the Holy Spirit reveals himself most faithfully through the text of Scripture in the first place. Whichever position you take, the role of the Christian community in determining the meaning of scriptural revelation should not be underestimated (the Protestant view of the shaping of the canon has a lot to do with our understanding of how God verifies truth through the believing community). Pulling together the strands of the above thoughts on the inspiration of God's revelation in Scripture, theologian Erickson makes these comments.

Postmodernism has reminded us, correctly, that we are not purely cognitive or rational creatures. Experience plays a major part in our understanding and our beliefs. From the perspective of evangelical Christianity, this means that the content of revelation is a deliverance wholly from God, but that the understanding of the revelation is affected and can be assisted by our experience of God's actually working in our lives. But what the kingdom of God says to us is that it is not merely the experience of individual Christians, or of an elite segment of the church, but of the entire, universal community, that helps us understand and apply that truth.'[33]

Remember Peter's warning: 'Above all, you must understand that no prophecy of Scripture came about by the prophet's own interpretation. For prophecy never had its origin by the will of man, but men spoke from God as they were carried along by the Holy Spirit' (2 Pet. 1:20–21). Implicit in this instruction is the principle that there is one meaning to each specific portion of Scripture, one intended by the Holy Spirit, and that it is up to the church, not the individual, to discern correctly. If you conclude with the apostle Peter that there are tracts of God's word whose meaning is not obvious (2 Pet. 3:16), especially when divorced from the collective wisdom, then there is a certain mystery and humility in handling God's word that is inherent – something that should smack of authenticity to the postmodern. In the same vein, the fact that the Greek NT preserves the textual variations of any given text in the footnotes should cause cynical postmodernists to derive greater confidence in the Christian Bible than in the Muslim Qur'an, which trots out one official, sanitized version. Christians are only interested in the search for truth, not in scoring points in some celestial gamesmanship.

Postmodernity is caught flat-footed. Claiming to be in the possession of a sacred and unerring text (in the original), the church does not pretentiously claim to know that truth exhaustively and perfectly, 'but that does not mean the only alternative is to disassociate text from speaker, and then locate all meaning in the reader or hearer'.[34] Christians admit not only that the individual is caught in the subjectivism of her or his own environment, but the church at any given moment, trapped in a cultural context, faces the same dilemma.

Nevertheless, as Bosch postulates: 'Our [the church's] theologies are partial, and they are culturally and socially biased. They may never claim to be absolutes. Yet this does not make them relativistic, as though one suggests that in theology – since we really cannot ever know 'absolutely' – anything goes ... Christians take seriously the epistemological priority of their classical text, the Scriptures.'[35]

Such relativism is partial and not absolute, then. Knowledge of God is possible through the Spirit illuminating the Scripture (1 Cor. 2:10). Christ the Son is knowable in the presence of his people (Mt. 18:20) and by the Spirit (Jn. 14:26). Martin Luther referred to this 'knowable' or plainly-apprehended quality of the Bible as *perspicuity*. This term comes from the Latin verb *perspicere* meaning 'to see through', and is the word from which we get *perspective*, again inferring an ability to understand with lucidity. God created us with the ability to communicate with each other through language and so it should not surprise us that, along with communicating to us about himself through the word made flesh, he also did so through the word penned in Hebrew, Aramaic, and Greek. Read as normal language, that is, in a literal fashion, as C.S. Lewis, among others, insists on, words taking their meaning from context, figures of speech being readily recognized as such and interpreted in that way, literary genre like poetry being allowed to follow their own rules of communication, and so forth, hence enabling the interpreter to master the clues and signals of the text so as to comprehend its true meaning, relatively easily, along with the help of the Holy Spirit, if not infallibly. This careful and humble approach to the text (including keeping in view historical theology, that is, the history of the church's engagement with the text) gives us every reason to believe that the self-disclosing

God has given us a trustworthy revelation of himself and what he wants us to know about how we should then live. Gnanakan, surrounded by a sea of religious pluralism in his native India, eloquently expresses the distinction we are making here: 'While accepting relativism as a reality, we will need to argue against the dogmatism of relativism as a philosophy ... We certainly need some authoritative reference point within the precarious position that pluralism pictures us to be in. That is why the revelation of Jesus Christ becomes even more crucial, when everything else is subjected to uncertainty.'[36]

While the radicalness of the word, properly understood in its absolute and yet conditioned state, ought to appeal to the postmodern mind in its own right, the remaining mystery of the most high God's infiniteness in relation to our finiteness intrigues and sparks a spiritual quest. While God is immanent (knowable, approachable, with us, especially through Jesus Christ (Jn. 1:14) and the indwelling Spirit), he is also transcendent (altogether other – Rom. 11:33). We cannot exhaust the riches (Col. 2:2–3) nor probe every aspect of the mysteries of who our self-disclosing and loving Father God is in this life (Jn. 21:25). But we know enough to know that we know truly (1 Jn. 1:1–3; Rom. 8:16).

An iron fist in a velvet glove

Concerning those of different faith or postmodern agnosticism, the way forward in effective witness to them is to practice all of the above *plus* offer our religious exclusivism with soft sell rather than hard sell, much as we say that some people on the surface seem placid and flexible, but underneath are insistent and unyielding; they have an iron fist in a velvet glove. In an age when style makes all the difference in the world, we must use gentler, user-friendly styles of communicating a pearl of great price that cannot be tampered with. Upon reflection, some of the gentle, peaceable and humble styles are woven into the gospel fabric itself; Jesus, for instance, did not force himself on anybody, pictured as not breaking a fragile reed (Is. 42:3), even though the consequences of people's not believing were unalterable and undesirable (Jn. 3:36).

The problem is that we initially present Christ as Saviour and Lord, but then, if his uniqueness is not grasped, for example in the course of friendship building with a Hindu, we then need to explain the fundamental differences between biblical Christianity and other faiths. The purpose of this book is not to defend this evangelical position, nor to engage in a treatise on comparative religion: however, it cannot be overstated that in our globalized, religiously plural, and postmodern world, we need to become skilled lay theologians with regard to world religions and savvy exegetes of postmodern culture.[37] But the problem is that while inherited wisdom, such as that from historian Arnold Toynbee, says that differences between religions relate to non-essentials and religions ultimately have a common essence, it does not take more than a cursory study of religions to see how radically different they are from each other. There are strands of similarity, such as the *bhakti* movement within Hinduism or the *Sufis* of Islam, which express devotion to personal Ram or Allah respectively, akin to the Christian concept of a personal God and creating us as persons, thereby enabling us to know him on an intimate level. As McGrath cogently argues, 'toleration is more likely to result from showing respect to other religions than from forcing them into an artificial framework that suppresses their distinctiveness in an attempt to make observation

conform to theory.'[38] Among other things, we have to
disabuse our audience of the notion that relativism is
necessary for the great diversity of beliefs that we are
only now becoming meaningfully aware of in the west.[39]
Nevertheless, conversely, 'we cannot possibly dialogue
with or witness to people if we resent their presence or
the views they hold ... Today few Christians anywhere
in the world find themselves in a situation where
coexistence with other religionists is not part and parcel
of their daily life.'[40]

There are several points of continuity with the
unsaved which enable us to treat them with respect and
dignity while being uncompromising in our discussions
with them about ultimate reality. At its core, attitudinal
tolerance begins with an acceptance that all humankind,
redeemed or fallen, is made in God's image (Js. 3:9).
Although distorted, innately found in humankind is a
seeking after God that is difficult to extinguish. Gnanakan
puts it this way: 'The basic fact we need to accept is
that within man is a capacity for knowing God and that
he seeks to know him through religion. Hence, rather
than condemning people within religion it is possible
to see that location as the very starting point for our
communication of the final claims of Christ for all the
world.'[41]

While rejecting attempts to show the sameness of
all religions – a misfiring missile at best – we must not
combatively stress the fundamental differences as our
first approach, but must appreciate what is laudable
in each faith while dialoguing with them about the
uniqueness of Jesus Christ. Kraus puts it well.

> There may be human and religious values in cultures
> outside the historical biblical tradition that excel those of
> our Western expressions. For example, we appreciate Inuit

sensitivity to nature, the Coptic respect for dignity and form in worship, the Islamic reverence for divine covenant law, the Buddhist regard for the wholeness of the cosmic order of which the individual is simply a part, and the traditional African respect for continuity through the generations.[42]

Persuasion with respect

Some might call this carrying an iron fist in a velvet glove hypocritical. I beg to differ. I call it reckoning with the fallenness of humankind. Pressing the delete button on fallenness is to take out the sense of urgency in our appeal and, in fact, to remove the persuasive element altogether. But sentiment turns to sledge hammer if we do not take into account being made in God's image. A gentler, softer apologetic is recommended by many students of religious pluralism, such as Fernando and Carson, recognized evangelical spokespersons of our day from two sides of the world. Reacting to the association of the spread of the gospel with colonialism in his native South Asia, Fernando is predictably against any proclamation that is triumphalistic or hints of a power display: 'Evangelists are servants. Colonialists are masters. Evangelists identify with the culture of others. Colonialists impose their culture upon others. Evangelists take up a cross of suffering upon themselves. Colonialists impose suffering on others.'[43] Applying his plea to our own context, what this Sri Lankan is calling for is the same humility attached to the persuasive witness described in 1 Peter 3:15: 'always be prepared to give an answer to everyone who asks you to give the reason for the hope that you have. *But do this with gentleness and respect*' [italics added].

Theologian Carson similarly urges for 'persuasion with respect' towards postmodernists and those from religions who will not take kindly to anything said with condescending or patronizing tones. In the midst of speaking and listening, we earn the right to hold to the following: 'However much we may defend the right of people to articulate their views, we must equally insist that some views are in error ... There is much likelihood of "serious and authentic dialogue" taking place between those who hold opposing positions, but who equally hold that objective truth is out there and is worth pursuing.'[44]

One simple yet effective way of engaging in non-threatening discussion when others say something like 'it's okay for you to believe in Christ, but why do I have to?' is to answer a question with a question. In this case, it might be something like 'What do you think? Would Jesus, if he were here today, expect you to believe in him?' Jesus frequently countered abrasive questions with ones of his own, as when the rich man asked him, 'Good teacher, what must I do to inherit eternal life?' (Mk. 10:17–8). Jesus replied, 'Why do you call me good?' That was not the end of the story, so we know that Jesus was not putting off the seeker by his initial question.

A soft hand inside the glove after all

I overstated my case above. True witness ushers out of genuine love for people. That's why Paul talks about Christ's love compelling him to be a missionary (2 Cor. 5:14). Have we not, upon our conversion, been enlarged in our hearts (not with heart disease!) with a newly found love for people? Our experience confirms the truth of Paul's statement that 'the love of God has been poured out within our hearts through the Holy Spirit who was given to us' (Rom. 5:5). Therefore we do not act like a hound waiting to pounce on the fox as we share our faith with those whom the Lord has led across our paths. We build authentic friendships with them. It is interesting to note that a recent investigation of churches thought to be missional discovered that a common feature of them was that they made a habit of inviting the stranger into the community as a welcomed guest.[45] Those of Asian-originating faiths and postmodern Generation X and Yers expect to relate to us at a deep level, where ongoing exchanges in the course of everyday living occur. Commenting on the new day of relational evangelism, Tiplady, himself from Generation X, says, 'Xers tend to share their faith more effectively when engaged in conversations that are 'two way', especially where personal beliefs, cultural philosophy and ideals are concerned: we value the other person's thoughts on faith issues as much as we want them to value ours.'[46] How can Muslims be expected to believe in a God who would demonstrate a kind of weakness by allowing his only son to be slain at the hands of an angry mob if they see no vulnerability or compassion in the way we relate to them; they are just waiting for their stereotypes about Christians at heart being people of *jihad*, of the Crusades, to be confirmed. We have an obligation to those of all races to 'speak the truth in love' (Eph. 4:15). This means, among other things, that we do not label other cultures as demonic and are careful about how we use spiritual warfare language.

Is there room for inter-faith dialogue?

Inter-faith dialogue is associated often with ecumenism or liberalism. In calling for a softer apologetics are we not in danger of losing our footing on a slippery slope by compromising the truth about Christ? If by *dialogue* we mean conceding to non-Christian convictions the same credibility and authority as our own, rather than simply giving them an equal opportunity to present their case, thus treating them respectfully, then dialogue is as useful as our appendix.

But there does seem to be room for dialogue in the witness of the early church. Note Paul's method of witness to the Athenians: 'So he reasoned in the synagogue with the Jews and the God-fearing Greeks, as well as in the market-place day by day with those who happened to be there (Acts 17:17).' The word *reasoned* here is a translation of a derivative from the verb, *dielegeto*, from which we get the English word *dialogue*. From the context, the dialogue obviously involved a dispassionate form of discussion, the next verse stating, 'A group of Epicurean and Stoic philosophers began to dispute ['were conversing', *NASB*] with him.' Verse 19 finds Paul being taken to the Areopagus to be granted an unusual opportunity for a hearing, in spite of some disagreement being evident in the previous discussion (v. 18b), but with the polite request being made, 'May we know what this new teaching is that you are presenting?' To say that Paul engaged in dialogue because he was ambivalent about the religious exclusivism that allegiance to Christ demanded is to ignore the framing of this evangelistic encounter, for we read in verse 16 that 'while Paul was waiting for them [Silas and Timothy] in Athens, he was greatly distressed to see that the city was full of idols.' Furthermore, the speech/preaching that segues from the dialogue (vv. 22–31) clearly has conversion as its goal, not to make people feel good about how tolerant they are toward each other. (Other uses of *dialogue* in Acts to denote this method of evangelism Paul used include 17:2; 18:4, 19; 19:9; 20:7, 9.)

Value added through the soft apologetics of dialogue, then, includes the following features:

- Interactive learning generally is more effective when people are not highly motivated to listen to a preaching monologue.
- Feedback from the audience helps us clarify how what we are saying is 'heard'.
- Dialogue does increase our opportunity to learn about the faith of others.
- Dialogue moves the passive hearer further along the continuum toward her or his will being challenged as emotions and reasoning skills are aroused.[47]

Cultural pluralists, not religious pluralists

Softer apologetics in a newly charged atmosphere of religious clashes or postmodern hypersensitivity about apparent intolerance may gain a fresh hearing for Christianity as non-believers see that we are cultural pluralists although not religious pluralists. Love in action is a sure way to win friends and influence people. Respectful but unyielding dialogue models how tolerance is not a function of *what* we believe but *how* we listen. Appreciating all people for their being made in God's image (while not whitewashing their fallenness) enables us to appreciate discriminatingly what is beautiful and brilliant in every culture – much in the way that Newbigin in speaking ahead of his time about Christian inclusivism, distinguished it from the unacceptability of religious pluralism: 'Cultural pluralism I take to be the attitude which welcomes the variety of different cultures and life-styles within one society and believes that this is an enrichment of human life.'[48]

Conclusion

As we soft-land the gospel, let us not forget, in review, of the apologetic of the believing community. Trotting

out propositional truth statements is no substitute for
the church living faithfully in the world as a credible
community. We have identified some of the ways that
testimony is lived out purely and therefore missionally.
Cynics are bred from watching more than listening, as
this exhortation shows.

> What our world is waiting for, and what the church seems
> reluctant to offer, is not more incessant talk about objective
> truth, but an embodied witness that clearly demonstrates
> why anyone should care about any of this in the first place.
> The fact that most of our non-Christian neighbors cannot
> pick us out from the rest of their non-Christian neighbors
> – or if they can, what makes us pick-outable are matters
> relatively incidental to the gospel – suggests that they are
> right in refusing to accept what we *say* we believe but which
> our *lives* make a lie.[49]

Nabila, one of North Africa's radiant Christians of the
past three decades, is emphatic in claiming that what
drew her to Christ was living in the home of a Christian
family from abroad and seeing over a period of time
how they really loved each other in a self-sacrificing way
– and that caused her to reflect on what they had been
telling her about divine, agape love. The evangelistic
potential of the church as a united, loving community has
not been fully realized even though it is explicitly taught
by our Lord: 'that all of them may be one, Father, just as
you are in me and I am in you. May they also be in us
so that the world may believe that you have sent me' (Jn.
17:21). In calling the church to chart the course for what
Newbigin calls 'an alternative plausibility structure', he
says, 'A plausibility structure is not just a body of ideas
but is necessarily embodied in an actual community.'[50] As
such, she demonstrates the validity of the theory, of the

story of God's intervention in history, ultimately through his Son: his story becomes Nabila's story, becomes our story. The book of Acts has been called the acts of the Holy Spirit through the early church. It ends at chapter 28 and in a sense the church today is writing chapter 29, as the Holy Spirit continues to accomplish God's mission on earth through the church until God's purposes on earth are consummated.

6. What the Borderless Church Looks Like: Mars Hill Community Church, US

The conclusion of the last chapter hints that it is time I put my money where my mouth is. Can I put a face to this theory of the borderless church? Let me tell you the story of Mars Hill Church – in my assessment, a missional church. As with any church appearing to be borderless, Mars Hill is in process. None of the churches profiled in this book would claim to possess all the qualities, much less the theology of a missional church. But they are part of the movement of the Holy Spirit enabling the church globally to rediscover her biblical roots of missionality just in kairos time to impact massively the twenty-first-century world.

I must confess that going to a church building which is a converted shopping mall never entered my imagination. I know of churches with an evangelistic meeting place in a mall or having a storefront presence. But taking over a whole mall? That was my experience in Grand Rapids, Michigan in the autumn of 2003 as I climbed out of the car of Pastor Keith Sparzak in a vast parking lot and headed inside the local mall with him to visit Mars Hill Church. The only thing was that the church took up the whole mall, which at one time featured 100 shops.

Let me push the reverse button a minute. I met Keith and a team of mission-minded people from his church by accident at a conference in a majority world nation in April 2003. They were visiting a church they were in partnership with and I was there to visit one of our workers connected with the same church. Over several days together we had several conversations and discovered that we had many similar views about the local church being missional in essence.

Keith began to tell me the remarkable story of a church that began in 1999 and yet is now frequented by ten thousand people.[1] What could fuel such phenomenal growth? Were the features found in Mars Hill those that had been identified by the research of German church growth expert Christian Schwartz, analysing thousands of churches on six continents, ones that he claimed lead to 'Natural Church Growth': empowering leadership, gift-oriented ministry, passionate spirituality, functional structures, inspiring worship services, holistic small groups, needs-oriented evangelism, and loving relationships?[2] Many of these self-same qualities are what I have been arguing will characterize the borderless church. Would Mars Hill demonstrate consistency with such findings?

The more I dug, the more I was startled to see the borderless nature of this church's core values. Keith's colleague on staff is David Stoner, senior missions' pastor at Mars Hill (Keith is his right-hand man), David's title actually being Lead Global Outreach (GO) Pastor. The church defines *global outreach* as 'the intentional advance of the gospel across cultural and language barriers beyond our church's normal boundaries of influence'.[3] Implicit in this self-understanding of the church and mission is that the mission field is everywhere, that the Arabs down the interstate highway (motorway) in Dearborn, Michigan are as much a part of the Mars Hill mission field as Arab Muslim counterparts in Lebanon and Yemen. Moreover, the disenchanted postmodern Generation X and Yers rejecting the institutional church in Dutch and Reformed Michigan around the corner are attracted to the church too. The Mars Hill website–(http://www.mhbcmi.org) not surprisingly, is user-friendly to post-Christian Erin.

You certainly get the impression of missional church as you visit their worship service on a Sunday morning – at least one of the several that will go on that day. Carved out of the centre of the mall is an amphitheatre with a stage in the middle. The place was abuzz and packed with three and a half thousand people on the morning I attended, the average age of attendee seeming to be twenty-five. Jeans and T-shirts were the order of the day. A contemporary band delivered the worship on a stage around which simple grey metal chairs fanned out in a 360 degree fashion. The teaching pastor, Rob Bell, dressed in open-necked shirt and trousers, looking to be no more than thirty (although he is older and in fact has a thorough formal theological education), roamed the platform talking in casual, down-to-earth tones, delivering a message full of personal anecdotes and peppered with stories as he artfully communicated the hope that there is in Jesus Christ. Interestingly, the teaching pastor is also part of a creative media initiative entitled 'Noomas'. Their productions are 12–15 minutes of MTV-quality videos designed to communicate in a manner that will connect with the contemporary culture and draw them to Jesus.

At any rate, that morning, there was little doubt that unchurched Sharon was hanging on every word. There was a transparency that was winsome. Sometimes in a Sunday testimony time they would have people share about their homosexual lifestyle or substance abuse, and disclose how this is what they were struggling with, or that is what God delivered them from. Instead of being scandalized, people applaud, affirm, lay hands on, and pray for them. One sensed a welcoming and healing community where the word of God is preached in unequivocal but relevant ways. Currently reshaping the language about the church, a statement drafted by the church's leadership and entitled 'Directions' hints at why such an atmosphere would be found in their worship services by declaring that 'we believe that God wants to redeem every part of us, and that Jesus's message of salvation is holistic in nature.' Keith summarizes their worship services as being 'where people are made to feel at home and allowed to see what God can do in their lives'.

Similarly the worship band that morning played with an edge and volume that would not alienate those unfamiliar with evangelical subculture, but that was worshipful nonetheless. The music was contemporary, and the band included penny whistle, drums, electric guitar, keyboards, harmonica, acoustic guitar, and lead and background vocals, enhanced by a superb sound system. A CD of their music entitled *Let the Door Stand Open* is suggestive of the way in which the church seeks to blend, thoughtfully, ministry to believers and non-believers alike. Included in the tribute on the sleeve of the CD to those involved in the project is a reference to 'the People out of every tribe and tongue', again, unobtrusively revealing how missionality is at the core of most things the church does.

This is one very evangelistic church – whether inside the mall walls or on the streets. The more I looked at this church the more I was convinced that her growth was due to her missionality. Mars Hill fits what Rick Warren referred to in defending the huge numbers attending his church: 'A church full of genuinely changed people attracts others. If you study healthy churches you'll discover when God finds a church that is doing a quality job of winning, nurturing, equipping, and sending out believers, he sends that church plenty of raw material.'[4]

The teaching pastor, Rob Bell, right from the beginning was thinking missionally. According to Keith

> They wanted a church that was going to be genuine, fresh, a healing community, one that connected well with a postmodern culture. They realized that what postmodern culture needed was the kind of transparency found in community and what makes a community a real community is mutual submission, humility, teachability, commitment to relationships, honesty and so forth ... It just carried itself over when we began to talk about global outreach. David [Stoner] and a small circle of others with a passion for global outreach started asking, 'What would a missional community look like and what are types of principles and practices that would be honouring to God that are a reflection of the overarching core values of Mars Hill and that could be incorporated into global outreach ministry?'

Maintains David, in a statement that is as missional as you can get, 'We, together with every spiritual leader in our spiritual community, are compelled by a shared sense of responsibility that the full measure of all the spiritual, human, and financial resources entrusted to us must be stewarded wisely in service of God's advancing kingdom.'[5]

Lest we cynics think that this is only the mission pastors shaping the conversation, look at the brochures visitors are introduced to as they come into the church mall. One is entitled 'BEYOND ME, BEYOND MARS HILL: becoming a global Jesus community'. In fact, they often refer to themselves, not by their formal name, but simply 'Mars Hill, a Jesus community'. No churchy jargon here.

Seamlessness

The word *seamless* keeps cropping up as you talk to Mars Hill folks. The more you listen and observe, the more you realize that it has everything to do with their drive to be a missional church. Keith intones: 'It refers to the intentional efforts that we are making to have ... a symbiotic relationship between the various ministry areas. The western church is notorious for compartmentalization ... We realized there is a certain necessity for [intentionality] when it comes to the missional calling of the church. We realized that the biblical model would be to have every ministry area have a missional mindset.'

This interweaving of mission into everything they do is seen in a multitude of ways. Take their children's ministry, for example. Cindy Bultema, the previous Children's Ministry Pastor, participated in an outreach to a refuge people group located in western Algeria. Later, a majority world church from a different country sent two people to observe and advise the children's ministry team at Mars Hill for two weeks. That connection in turn spurred Cindy into deciding to take 16 of her key ministry leaders to the overseas church for cross-cultural outreach. The result of this inculcating of world vision led to the children's ministry leadership team of Mars Hill rewriting their curriculum so that it better reflected the church's growing commitment to global mission. They have since taken up themes in the children's ministry like 'Global Disciple-Makers'. A component is built into the teaching which comes with weekly assignments like collecting notebooks and school supplies for an inner city school. Cindy's husband also served as Mars Hill's liaison between the children's ministry and global outreach, so the seamlessness began to be seen at work.

Similarly, one of their Community Life pastors led a work project in Morocco. An Administrative Services Director went to a North African Church conference in Malta two years ago. She then understood better why the cheques she writes for the Global Outreach Team are so important. The teaching pastor, Rob, was taken by David to South Africa because Rob already had a heart compassion for those with HIV/AIDS and this exposure only widened his eyes to see the larger problem globally. His trip has resulted in Mars Hill moving beyond her initial sense of being called in global mission to focus on North Africa to do ministry in sub-Saharan Africa, where the AIDS crisis is more pronounced.[6] Locally, the church participates in and is an advocate of the Grand Rapids AIDS Walk in cooperation with the Grand Rapids AIDS Task Force. An AIDS Ministry Team has been formed to flesh out the church's discerning that she should be a problem solver locally and globally in this gargantuan fight.

Listen to David talk about how seamlessness represents one of the church's core values: 'This concept emphasizes our commitment to the kind of interdependence and synergy in our GO vision and strategy that overcomes the usual barriers that divide and separate the various ministry arenas of a local church.'[7] As we have been seeing, that integrated philosophy of ministry is a sign of a church being missional.

Missional house churches

My first night there I met some of those radically changed people at a home group meeting. Many of the fifteen or so adults present had been saved no longer than the life span of the church. They came out of traditional denominations. They came from broken marriages. They were disillusioned at the institutional Protestant church in some cases. Some were young and hip. They were a typical group, I was told.

Initially the small group ministry was modelled after Willow Creek's. But in the last few years the leadership of the church realized that they wanted more of a house church type of small group instead of just having a Bible study and some occasional times of deep sharing. An Acts-like model engendered grass roots caring, leading of new followers of Jesus through discipling to baptism, and things like baby dedications. These small groups, then, function somewhat as churches within a larger church. Devolving to the micro-unit enables more of their attendees to take on ministry responsibilities, to discover and develop their spiritual gifts. Exclaims Keith, 'When we have [new] opportunities to do different ministries, we put them through the network of house churches ... and invite them [to get involved]. Our goal is to have our house churches provide the support for our international and local partners in a real personal level.'

If you look at the informational flyers found at the kiosks dotting the church mall corridors, they encourage visitors or those beginning to get involved in the church to view the small groups as house churches. The flyer related to small groups is headed with the catchphrase *Yes! I want to be in Biblical Community!* Underneath this introduction is the instruction: *Please complete the following information and someone from Mars Hill Community will connect you with a House Church.*

Hence, Mars Hill home church groups are able to provide most of the range of 'works of service' (Eph. 4:11-12) viewed as essential by those involved in cell church propagation:

- support for new believers;
- need-meeting interpersonal relationships;

- spawning of lay leaders;
- abiding in Christ in community;
- accessible opportunities for evangelism and ministry.[8]

As we have contended throughout, a missional church in a postmodern context will stress and exemplify community. In the Mars Hill website 'About Us' page, they state that growth and healing on the individual level can occur in community. Similarly, they attribute their growth not to their team of pastors, leaders, and staff, but the involvement of the community members – or 'the people in the grey chairs' as they like to refer to the non-paid staff. Moreover, in their 'Directions' statement, the emphasis on community as a core value comes through in the words 'we believe that we were created to live deeply with one another, to carry each others' burdens and share our possessions, to pray for and confess our sins to each other, to suffer and to celebrate together. It's in these sacred relationships and honest, loving communities that God transforms us.'

Community is not an exercise in navel-gazing, however. Their website page on 'Community Life' includes these two astounding statements showing the seamless flow between inward-looking ministry (that is, community-building through small groups) to outward-looking ministry: 'At Mars Hill our vision is "to make disciples who make disciples" by encouraging and facilitating people to move from "observation" to active participation through commitment to service …' and 'We … are committed to excellence in all that we do and desire to be a part of the great game plan for the nations as they come to the Kingdom of God.'

A glocal perspective on mission

Noting the schizophrenia that is the rule rather than the exception when it comes to understanding the geographical parameters of mission, Stoner remarks, 'It is not uncommon for a local church to operate separate local and international (the further away from the church the more valid) outreach programs, often under the oversight of different ministry divisions. At the very least, this built-in dichotomy in a local church's outreach saps the vitality and strength of its overall missional impact.'[9]

In fact, Mars Hills' GO ministries are organized into local and global categories, but under one roof. David oversees both departments. Passionately communicating this glocal vision of mission, David declares: 'In these definitional and structural ways, we are purposefully moving our GO model away from compartmentalization and the competing interests it can breed, toward greater complementarity and cohesion. This is the ethos that drives our vision of "the new kind of church in the world" we feel called to fulfil: *a seamless missional community.*'[10]

While the church has felt led to a concentration on North Africa (Arab outreach), East and South Africa (HIV/AIDS), and Southeast Asia in its global ministries, not wanting to dilute its potential impact in any one area of the most unreached expanses of the planet, they view the local outreach programmes as ideal classrooms to determine individuals' spiritual gifts, character development readiness, and calling to international service. Thus David persuasively states, 'Ultimately, we envision this *glocal* synergy of experiential equipping and serving opportunities to be both the point of departure and destination for every Mars Hill GO servant. A *seamless* local and international developmental process suggests the promise of a learning cycle in which global disciple makers are expected to both receive and give back.'[11]

Their local ministries are linked philosophically and strategically to their international foci. For example, among the emerging local ministry platform is a welcoming of strangers in ministering to the practical needs of Muslim refugees, deliberate befriending of Muslim international students, and a programme to learn Arabic. Typical of Mars Hills' commitment to reach out to the unchurched and needy around them is their Christmas Project that involves things like adopting a poor family over the holiday. Food and other gifts help such families not feel that Christmas is a sad time of the year. Gift certificates or food baskets can be donated for those people who do not feel they can get too personally involved with a needy family over the festive season. Another project sees church folk providing books and school supplies to an inner city school whose parents cannot compensate for the lack in government provision.

But let's not ignore Mars Hill's thrust into the regions beyond. Listed in the *2004 Service Opportunities* are five short-term mission opportunities, all overseas. The first is *Serving Sahrawi*, referring to those in the former Spanish Sahara territory (disputed land in the west of Morocco) and provided ministry opportunities for teaching in their refugee camps in Algeria.[12] Again, though, we see the integrated, or seamless, approach to building world Christians as being alongside the cross-cultural experience through their local summer sponsorship programme, a *Praying through the 10/40 Window* possibility for involvement, a Samaritan's Purse Christmas shoebox ministry, political advocacy, and a Ramadan prayer focus.

Other mission opportunities include this same blending of localized and geographically distant components. They centred on literature distribution in Morocco, a motorcycle prayer journey in Tunisia, a summer children's outreach in Egypt, construction and maintenance projects in Malta, and numerous adult and children's outreaches in Spain to Arab immigrants. This church has determined strategically to focus her overseas ministry in a region of the world where Christ is least known and the church is least present (Rom. 15:20). Mars Hill is not focused on black Africa, where ministry comes more easily (except where it involves their HIV/ AIDS and associated justice initiatives) but where the church could arguably be sending missionaries their way, or on Latin America, where the same growth makes questionable the western world's continued tradition of sending missionaries in that direction, as if the continent was, in effect, as unevangelized as it was in 1900. An increasingly missional church does not haphazardly engage in cross-cultural ministry (although any exposure is better than none in moving a church in meaningful global mission) but looks where the need is the greatest unless clearly called to a specific ministry where the church is already strong. This spirit of going where no one else is going is captured in their oft-quoted slogan, *'There are no God-forsaken places in the world … just church-forsaken.'* Interestingly, a narrow niche ministry to the unreached is perceived by Generation X missiologists as being attractive to the younger generation seeking to make their lives count for eternity.[13]

Engaging young people in reaching out in social and verbal ways to the lost locally and globally is working. It explains why the Saturday night home meeting Keith and Suzanne organized for me in their home for only those who had been to North Africa and were praying about being involved there in the future in some sort of long-term capacity was packed. About 40 young adults (and several 'builders'[14]) crowded into their home and probed me with informed and penetrating questions about God's will, the nature of ministry in the Arab world, and our mission agency. Is this sort of church dynamic not what we are told to expect in a missional church by those tracking such trends? 'Every Christian community should see itself as a community of missionaries. Its responsibility ... is to guide them to identify God's calling, to recognize the gifts and opportunities they have, to provide them with the biblical and theological training to incarnate the gospel in their particular fields, and then to commission them to that ministry. Our structures of membership need to be transformed into disciplines of sending.'[15]

One senses a great deal of convergence in Mars Hill about what it means to be borderless as a church, not limiting their sense of identity and purpose to what occurs inside the many walls of a mall. Instead, they are swept away by the breathtaking vistas of God's plan of rescue and blessing for the nations. Now, that's a borderless church.

7. Borderless Churches and the Continuing Scandal of the 10/40 Window

Coming out of the movie theatre in Amman, Jordan, as crowds emptied from the showing of *The Passion of the Christ* into the shimmering heat of the summer of 2004, a teenager was overheard asking her veiled and black robed mother, 'Look at how much Jesus suffered on the Cross for us. Why are we told he did not die?'

'Shh', whispered her mother, 'we'll talk about it when we get home.'

This inquisitive girl was but one of millions of the 1.3 billion Muslims worldwide who went to this graphic, powerful portrayal of the sufferings of Christ expecting to see a Mel Gibson action film (who says branding doesn't work) and an anti-Semite film, but who would normally not publicly endorse any movie that reinforced the Christian teaching that Christ actually died. Muslims, of course, deny the deity and death of Christ although they acknowledge his historicity, that he was a prophet and sinless. Thrilling it was to see God's providential sovereignty opening the way for tens of millions of Muslims to gain exposure to the true gospel story of the death and resurrection of Christ, and in an art form that would speak penetratingly to their hearts. On the other hand, it exposes the little-known reality of a world closeted from the truth, like an archaeological artefact revealed by soil erosion. Like the archaeology hidden from view, the unreached world lies largely untouched and unnoticed until something unusual happens in it.

Ignorance is bliss

What do you do about the over three thousand people groups without a viable indigenous church, chiefly in what has been labelled the 10/40 Window of North Africa, the Middle East, and Asia, when your Generation X churchgoer may subscribe covertly to the 'wider hope' conviction that Jesus is but one way of many?[1] Or how is the church's missionality to make a difference when one in seven North Americans can't even locate the US on a world map, let alone remote Mauritania, Muslim and Arab for over a millennium, where there are only eight known underground, struggling, indigenous churches? Who will give up double latte coffees when they remain blissfully ignorant of the fact that 2.4 billion people, again largely in the 10/40 Window, live on less than two dollars a day?[2] In a Euro-American obsession with consumerism that finds evangelicals with less time and less discretionary money than ever, can we expect sensitivity to the fact that a Nike quilted jacket costs £100 in a High Street shop, but only 51 pence of that goes to the Bangladeshi woman making it? Or that the top 1 per cent of households in the US has more wealth than the bottom 95 per cent?[3] Scathing in her analysis of the church, Harris contends: 'If I and my local congregation are calling ourselves Christian, but we live under the rule of money, how can we call Noelle to choose the Jesus way to the exclusion of other spiritual paths … the West is constructed around the biblical lie that we can divide the spiritual and the secular, the religious and the nonreligious', which she argues explains the fact that there has been a 60 per cent drop on giving since 9/11, something that has a bearing on the condition of the least evangelized nations on earth. 'Where is our security?' she rhetorically asks.[4]

One is mystified that there should yet be so many unreached people groups when the spread of the gospel down through church history has created the conditions listed below:

* In AD 100 there were about twelve unreached people groups for every church.
* In 1900 there were about ten churches for every unreached people group.
* In 2000 there were at least six hundred churches for every unreached people group.[5]

Ignorance is bliss, but what about misinformation?

The following misleading emphases discourage the church in the west from continuing to send missionaries to least-reached peoples of the globe.

* **Glib triumphalism from the pulpit that focuses on the fact that there are known believers in every one of the 238 nations of the world, identifiable Christians found in about 11,500 of the 12,600 ethno-linguistic peoples of the globe, and Christians who can share their faith in 12,500 of the world's 13,500 distinct languages.**[6] Such facts are great causes of rejoicing and point to the 'success' of the missionary movement of the past two hundred plus years. But *only* stressing the positives misleads a somewhat missiologically illiterate church that largely remains

oblivious to the reality that in too much of the planet that river of Christian presence flows a mile wide and an inch deep. Yes, there are Muslim background believers (MBBs) in Libya as opposed to none three decades ago, but, at the time of writing, we only know of 34 of them, and none are gathered into an underground national worshipping group.

The result of failing to add texture to the picture painted is a reductionism that leaves people in the pews concluding that the greatest need is here in the pagan and post-Christian west. Meanwhile, 27 per cent of the world's population is estimated to have never heard the gospel.[7] Part of this glossing over of fine distinctions of 'reached' and 'unreached' is the estimate that fewer than 10 per cent of churches in the western world have a mission committee. If a church fails to develop lay specialists in missiology, can it expect to be conversant with such concepts as 'a church found within a people group or nation has the inherent capacity to reach its own people without outside help once the evangelical proportion of its population has reached a critical mass of 2 per cent or more'?

An additional source of malaise caused by focusing too much on the success stories of world evangelization is that, somehow, the closer we get to the finished task, the more de-motivating it can be to complete the job. One church leader describes the lack of incentive this way: 'We have moved the ball [using an American football image] from deep in our territory to the opponent's two-yard line – we think – and the last few inches don't inspire us as much.'[8]

- **Indiscriminate involvement of the local church in direct church-to-church engagement with those in traditional mission fields, instead of developing**

strategic deployment of limited human and financial resources to the most unreached. None of the four churches profiled in this book is guilty of 'throwing good money after bad'. However, in both surveys of UK churches in the *Connect!* series, Tim Jeffrey documents how churches got involved in places like Kenya, Uganda, and Brazil – all countries with populations massively more evangelized than Great Britain – as their starting point in overseas mission.[9] Guns on the ramparts of the forts are fixed in the same old directions when it comes to thinking about where missionaries and money should be sent. Sometimes mission links come about somewhat accidentally, as when contact is made in the church in Nigeria because a Nigerian attended a western church while studying abroad. With eased communication and travel, it is not surprising that such links develop, and at least it puts mission on the agenda of the local church. The downside is that any engagement in cross-cultural ministry overseas will only be strategic involvement in mission if the church's initial exposure to the larger world of need is a launching pad to *a primary focus on the 815 people groups currently without any witness along with the other more than 2000 people groups that can be classified as unreached, unless there is an unmistakable calling to a different and pressing cross cultural involvement, such as alleviating AIDS in sub-Saharan Africa.*[10] Should we make such distinctions? I will let missionary statesman, Lesslie Newbigin have the last word for now (this issue will be considered further in Chapter 9).

We must understand the purpose and goal of missions. I am using the word 'missions' in distinction from the more all-encompassing word 'mission'. This latter word I take to mean the entire task for which the Church is sent into the world. By 'missions' I mean those specific activities which are undertaken by human decision to bring the gospel to places or situations where it is not heard, to create a Christian presence in a place or situation where there is no such presence or no effective witness.[11]

The problem in thinking about mission holistically (local and global together, for example) is that it can blur some important distinctions that inform effective strategy for engagement in mission by the local church.

• **Ignoring statistical realities about the unreached world in favour of heart-tugging stories and emotional appeals about the latest natural disaster.** (This is not to downplay that God looks on each individual with such compassion that we dare not reduce mission to a statistical chart.) Notwithstanding that corrective, I must say how I remember being struck at Urbana, the IVCF tri-annual missions' conference, which I attended as a university student in 1970, by the simple but telling analogy of the see-saw in relation to deciding where to go as a missionary. 'If you were invited to balance out the teeter totter, when there were nine people on one end and one on the other, which end would you go to?' was compared to getting involved in ministry to least-reached peoples as opposed to giving ourselves to reaching people for Christ where the church was strongest. That concept became a building block for my ultimate calling to reach least-reached peoples, something that has never left me. Therefore, to be frank, I am dismayed to find that 97 per cent of missionary deployment (long- or short-term) is still in the 141 countries where the population is 61 per cent or more Christian.[12]

• **A jingoism that says 'let the nationals do it and we'll just send the money and prayers.'** As I documented in an earlier book, *We Are the World: Globalisation and the Changing Face of Missions*, it is exciting to see how the Lord has raised up an army of majority world missionaries that may soon outnumber those from the western world.[13] For example, at the COMIBAM conference of Latino missions in October 1997, results of a survey were released that found that there were 397 agencies and 3498 missionaries from Latin America.[14] That being said, the remaining global task is so mammoth that it will take the full mobilization of the worldwide church to reach the whole world for Christ in our generation. As I write, I am days away from heading to Nigeria to speak at a conference of an indigenous mission agency, CAPRO, which has 430 missionaries and staff ministering mostly in sub-Saharan Africa. Yet they have rarely sent any workers to the Arab world, where the spiritual need is more pronounced. CAPRO is starting a partnership agreement with AWM whereby they will send workers through us, as they feel the idea of doing it alone quite daunting. Notwithstanding these encouraging developments from new sending churches, once local churches in the US, the UK, or Canada start sending money only (because it is cheaper to support a national) they start down the slippery slope that leads to doing the Great Commission by proxy and to a shrivelling of the mission vision that we contend is at the core of what church is all about. A keen mission observer puts the whole issue in perspective for us with these words: 'I sometimes wonder if we aren't falling thoughtlessly into the trend of exporting jobs overseas to take advantage of cheap labour – a trend with definite short-term economies but with long-term consequences that warrant more attention.'[15]

- **Sending of short-term missionaries is put on the same level of effectiveness as fielding long-term missionaries who learn the language, and who, in a word, are the only ones becoming incarnational.** Can you believe that the US alone sends 1 million short-term missionaries a year in the early years of the twenty-first century and yet only 50,000 career missionaries, that is, 5 per cent of their total harvesting force?[16] Too superficially, that initial short-term exposure, as life-changing as it can be, is passed off as 'doing my bit for mission'. Furthermore, it can have the result of detrimentally driving long-term strategy. Can the church really be planted among Bhojpuri-speaking Dalits in Uttar Pradesh by those who do not master the largely illiterates' heart language and customs? In the meantime, short-term mission gobbles up the lion's share of financial resources for global mission. A sample study of one Central American country revealed that over $10 million a year were being spent on short-term trips to that country alone.[17] This trend has produced such side-effects as church staff and mission pastors becoming regular frequent flyer members.[18]

- **Overplaying the view that 'everybody is a missionary' undercuts the recognition that there is a special calling for certain individuals in the church to become cross-cultural specialists and communicators of the gospel.** Miley puts it this way: 'The well-intended idea that "everybody should be a missionary" violates this truth [that] God in his wisdom made generous provision in the Church for a rich diversity of natural abilities, spiritual gifts, and learned expertise. Trying to make everybody the same disregards Christ's headship of the Church.'[19] Long-term missionaries to the spiritually-neglected and gospel-resistant stretches of the 10/40 Window in the Muslim, Hindu, Sikh, and Buddhist worlds will require those who stick around for the long haul and should form the backbone of any missional church's strategy for reaching the lost 'over there'. Those kinds of missionaries need a special calling, in my opinion, in a way that everyone sharing their faith in their own workplaces and neighbourhoods does not. Both species of Christians are missionaries. But those crossing many barriers, whether they are geographical, linguistic, or cultural, are a specialist breed of missionary. They will need linguistic skills, cultural adaptability, and relational strengths that enable the Holy Spirit to break down barriers in the receptor culture. Experience teaches me that one will not stick it out for long in such a ministry and context without being set apart and sent out by a local church as a result of a mutually-recognized calling. Moreover, discipleship must follow conversion, and discipleship involves community. In other words, can short-termers really plant the church and nurture maturing believers in the context of an indigenous, fledgling church? Of course not. Growing communities of disciples where the gospel has not taken root, in the Hindu, Buddhist, Sikh, and Muslim worlds, implies a skill set for the missionary (and national) that is forged in the crucible of experience, identification with the culture, and the heart-ache of slow, arduous work. Agreed, the Holy Spirit surprises and breaks out in ways we cannot predict; but we cannot make the exceptions the basis for establishing a rule; in this case, 'let's do mission through short-termers because the Holy Spirit is not limited to long-term missionaries.'

- **Assuming that our local church's heightened involvement in global mission absolves us of needing to support parachurch mission specialists.** Sad it is to note that many majority-world Christians perceive Christians in the west as wealthy people who build concrete block houses worldwide.[20] While it could be argued that career missionaries are expensive, it is difficult to put a premium on the great value of someone who has mastered the local language, has a servant heart, and is contextualizing the gospel in a people group where the first churches are struggling to take root. Even more appalling is to discover that many such missionaries struggle to attract an adequate financial (let alone prayer!) following: the drop in value of the American dollar vis-à-vis international currencies post 9/11 has forced many career missionaries to spend inordinate amounts of time in their homeland shoring up their support base instead of training local national leadership in how to plant churches or serving as advocates for justice for widows and orphans in HIV/AIDS-ravaged nations. Add to that reality, to take American Christians only (already known for their generosity), less than six per cent of them tithed in 2003 and there has been a 60 per cent drop in giving since 9/11, so is it any wonder that there are still three thousand unreached peoples scattered around the world?[21]

One more thought while we develop this bullet point: as much as we applaud the formation of borderless churches as we enter the twenty-first century, the reality is that for every-one of those that is emerging there is a score of those which are self-absorbed. One pastor put it this way: 'We need another concert, anther seminar, another Christian television station – quickly! Who was it who said, "The greatest threat to world evangelism is the church preoccupied with her own existence"?'[22]

The sense of hopelessness versus bright possibilities

One of my bleakest reads of late was on the airplane from Heathrow to Lagos and back again after a week of ministry in Nigeria. I met Claire, Dag, and Andy living in the arid wasteland of Palm Springs, California in *Generation X*. Their sense of hopelessness and world-weary cynicism is captured in Andy's retort to middle-aged, materialistic Margaret, a neighbour: 'God, Margaret. You really have to wonder why we even bother to get *up* in the morning. I mean, really: *Why work*? Simply to buy more *stuff*? That's just not enough. Look at us all.'[23]

It is not just non-believing postmoderns who are filled with a sense of hopelessness about the future. Evangelical young people are searching for meaning too and are somewhat confused. Paula Harris, a leader of the Urbana tri-annual mission conference sponsored by IVCF between Christmas and New Year since the late 1940s and attended by 20,000 university students, observes about those who now come

> Missions may not be in their vocabulary, but they are searching for their 'mission in life' … Fifty-two percent come to Urbana to learn about missions. Seventy-five percent come to Urbana simply to seek God's will for their lives. Somehow, in this context of listening to Bible teaching and missionary speakers, praying for the world, worshiping God and being open to the Holy Spirit's leading, many students are directed by God to make significant missions commitments.[24]

The sense of rootlessness in Generations X and Y has been pointed out by mission observers for a few years now. The lament is that, suspicious of authority figures and institutions, and betrayed too often by the breakdown of familial relationships, these young adults are unwilling to make long-term commitments to cross-cultural mission. This characterization has been one theory to explain the explosion of short-term mission. But recent evidence unearthed by the World Evangelical Alliance Missions Commission's 20 nation study on missionary retention (ReMAP II) reveals that the average length of tenure for the worst retaining agencies is seven years, and for the best retaining ones seventeen years.[25] This augurs well for the future wave of those taking the gospel to least reached peoples, primarily in the 10/40 Window.

Speaking as one such Generation Xer, Brit, Rob Hay, pleads, 'We Xers are committed to long-term missions (20 years plus) – but it is unlikely to be with one organization and if it is to be with your organization you have to be prepared to build trust and not just expect to have it from day one.'[26] Indicative of this generational turnaround is a UK movement seeking to mobilize 10,000 16–25-year olds into local and global mission. Called Motiv8, it seeks 'to make it easier for young people to think and do mission'. It is built around a yearly event, the first one held in 2004 in Manchester (see www.what4.org.uk/motive8-for details).

Conclusion

The phenomenon of teenagers riding the crest of the wave of short-term mission is encouraging. OM's Teen Street is enlisting Missionary Kids and their friends to hear afresh the challenge of Christ to lay down their lives for him and for the gospel's sake. Groups like Teen Mission mobilize thousands of already world-weary kids every summer. Young people are searching for meaning besides climbing up the property ladder, as witnessed by Joel from Generation X: 'Time is a precious commodity to my generation. If you convince me that something's worth my time, however, you will suddenly find my attention span is no longer a problem.'[27] May that passion for meaning in life translate to overcoming the scandal of the 10/40 Window's neglect by churches that are searching for what it means to be borderless.

8. What the Borderless Church Looks Like: New Life Church, Worthing, England

Three images flash through my mind about New Life Church as I seek to put a face on missional churches in the UK. The first image is of a multitude of flags suspended from the ceiling as nations are prayed for Sunday mornings. The second is of a baptismal service in which an ex-convict, a recovering alcoholic, a former gambler, and the child of a single parent were among those baptized, all won through the ministry of the church in the community. The third is of grateful smiles on the faces of the elderly and homeless gathered for a Christmas Day dinner put on by the church.

New Life Church (NLC) is proof that you do not have to be a big church to be missional. Of the four churches featured in this book, NLC, in the 'retirement capital' of England, not far from Brighton on the English Channel, devotes 30 per cent of their budget to mission, and has a proven track record in the community, including through planting four churches. If current Sunday morning attendance is any gauge, it looks like they will have to plant another one soon, or go to multiple services. Hardly a seat in the 200-seat sanctuary is free any Sunday morning, with an overflow crowd seated in an adjoining hall. Many attendees are people from the community who have been saved or continue to seek after God as a result of participating in Alpha courses or other programmes mounted by NLC.

A little history helps

The year 2005 marks this Baptist Union church's centenary year, for it was in the spring of 1905 that a few local Christians in the Worthing suburb of Durrington began an upper room meeting in a house on Stone Lane. A church gradually formed; minutes of deacons' and church meetings trace back to 1911 at which time a plot of land had been purchased, the building being completed for £380 in 1912.[1] In 1939, the existing church building was added to the original one, which now serves as the Coffee Shop.[2] In response to continual prayer for revival that began in 1966, the first significant spiritual breakthrough began in the autumn of 1972 when Campbell McAlpine came to conduct special meetings. In a quiet way initially, many hearts were stirred and the Holy Spirit began to move amongst the church members. Without going into the history of the ensuing revival, suffice it to say that a passion to reach the lost locally and globally was generated during those years. Many people were added to the church, to the extent that NLC felt ready to send out 40 adults in 1981 to plant a new church in another part of town, the new church then called Broadwater Christian Fellowship. Three more churches were planted in the next decade in West Sussex County, indicative of the church's responsiveness to the Holy Spirit (most churches would simply grow into bigger buildings or extra services) and her missional heart.

Home groups are part of the strategy

Presently there are 20 home groups. The home group my wife and I attend has about 16 adults in it. The hosts display remarkable warmth toward new Christians and are committed to lifestyle evangelism, as are several other leaders of home groups. Not surprisingly, many of those in our group are fairly new believers. Occasionally unsaved family members or friends are made to feel welcome at a garden barbeque or Christmas buffet dinner. Some of the regulars are graduates of the Alpha programme (in fact several home groups have formed after Alpha courses). Their enthusiasm for the Lord rubs off on the rest of us.

During the autumn of 2004, the number of groups doubled for a season as the church corporately went through *The Purpose Driven Life*. Seekers and lapsed church attendees were attracted by the structured, straightforward approach, one that was user-friendly for the unchurched. In the long term, the groups are intended to follow a curriculum that ties in with the Sunday teaching. This intentionality and mobilizing of the laity through home groups contribute to the missionality of NLC. On the church website the purpose of the home groups is described this way: 'Through the varied activities of the groups we want to become better equipped to serve Jesus as well as making our unique gifts available for the benefit of the wider community. People are "pastored", gifts are used, potential leaders are identified, and trained. Ultimately, members' spiritual lives are enhanced so that the Kingdom becomes stronger.'

Global mission: an extension of local mission

The lead statement of the church on global mission is revealing: 'It is recognized that as individuals are called, so the Church also is called to go into all the world.

New Life Church is both a sending Church and a going Church. Inasmuch as churches worldwide are involved in the Great Commission, this is a task in which we all share as partners.' Not surprisingly, about 30 per cent of the church budget goes to local and global mission. This is the dividing line that some students of churches and mission say separates the men from the boys.[3]

What strikes you about NLC in her mission focus is the fluidity of money and movement of personnel between local and global commitments. Several missionaries have been sent out from the church, such as Rachel Bass serving in Russia. Others have been adopted over the years, such as Vickie Blair, ministering in Kyrghyzstan, who recently became more England-based and took over pastoring one of NLC's church plants. Furthermore, others, like Jan Rowland and Mintie Nel, are based in Worthing, involved normally in the life of the church, but come and go to carry out a ministry to single missionaries in places like Hungary. All have been embraced with open arms. There has been no wariness about the church being overextended financially, even if there is a mature critical thinking brought to bear on where and how the church should steward her financial resources. Graham Jefferson, the senior pastor, with conviction, insists that New Life has long believed that she has been called to be a major force in world mission and has repeatedly reminded the church of needing to be a house of prayer for the nations (Mt. 21:13). The pastor and other leaders periodically go to visit their missionaries and promote cross-cultural short-term mission programmes.

Most telling about NLC's servant heart for the peoples of the planet is her evolving interest in supporting nationals. For example, they support two Brazilian missionaries in Poland, two Romanian nationals, Chileans church planting in Madrid, and Brazilians in

Israel and Egypt. Supporting nationals is most visibly expressed, though, by the running of Arrows Language School, birthed several years ago out of a desire to cater for the growing number of mostly YWAM majority world people coming to the UK to learn English before heading on to an unreached people, usually in the 10/40 Window. Students come for six months or one year of language acquisition and are hosted in homes of church members. Frequently under-funded, these nationals end up being supported materially by church members in one way or another.

Members of the church are encouraged to follow through with their own vision for cross-cultural service, such as John Ray who has set up a ministry in the last year sponsoring the education of 15 Ugandan children. Members of the church also head up the work of local charities such as Link Romania, involved in relief work. The influence of the church gets extended to lifelong networks of relationships that never make a budget line in the church's financial statements.

On the home front, Edward is a stunning example of the lives of those the church is touching through outreach ministries like Alpha. He turned from a life of substance abuse and crime to find his spiritual feet in New Life Church. With his pony tail, weather-worn face, and jeans, he brings fresh enthusiasm and an air of reality to church life. But Alpha is only the tip of the iceberg of a borderless church in action. *Jubilee Nursery* is run on week-day mornings by four qualified staff; they have 26 neighbourhood children under their care. Some of the unchurched parents have responded to opportunities for counselling over marital difficulties or the challenges of rearing children in single-parent homes. *Whizz Kids* is a mid-week club for children age five to ten, taking place on a Wednesday in Jubilee Hall, the all-purpose facility owned by the church and across the road from the main building. An average of 25 kids from a mix of church and community homes comes every week for a combination of games and biblical input. *Entity* welcomes 20 teenagers, some of whom took part in London in the 2004 summer, inter-church outreach called 'Soul in the City'. *Jubilee Club* is a year old, birthed to provide friendship, acceptance, and belonging for about 30 isolated adults in the community. *Coffee Shop* opens twice weekly and reaches many unchurched friends from the community. Elderly folk enjoy a free bus service to the nearby superstore and then stay for lunch. A number of customers have joined an Alpha course, some even getting converted and added to the church.

In the summer, many from the church are mobilized to run a booth at the local festival, offering free refreshments to passers-by and give-aways for children while being available in a low-key way to talk to people about Christ or invite them to church services or activities. Church members are heavily involved in the Worthing churches' Homeless Project. Alison Gurney manages the Direct Access Hostel and some 20 New Life volunteers regularly help in some aspect of the ministry. The largest AA chapter in the area meets on church premises. NLC are very community-focused as an expression of their missional intentionality.

The centrality of the word

One of the things attracting my wife and me to worship at New Life, first having checked out six different churches in Worthing, was the high calibre of preaching evidenced in Graham Jefferson's pulpit ministry. Blessed with more of a teaching-feeding gifting than exhortational-evangelistic, Graham's style balances nicely the freer worship emphasis of much of the rest of the Sunday morning worship services. Sometimes charismatic practice is disassociated from sound teaching; such is not the case at NLC. The Holy Spirit has been at work marvellously for decades in this church, but as their previous pastor says, 'Holy Spirit renewal will always bring a fresh love and appreciation of the word of God.'[4]

Two things indicate the missionality of the church's focus on the Scriptures. One is the way the Word is preached so as to enable the congregation to catch a vision for the purpose of the church in the world. The 2004 series on *The Purpose Driven Life* tied the word preached, the praises sung, and the home group material studied around the same theme: to establish believers in foundational biblical living. The word is expected to change lives and shine a searchlight on the future of the church's ministries. Second, is the stress on the formation of discipleship groups. About 75 per cent of the church's membership has gone through discipleship group training since March 2002.

The winsomeness of the worship

Unusual it may be to find a church website devoting so much space to worship and prayer, but it is a true reflection of priorities at NLC. Introducing the praise and worship pages on the website is this statement:

> New Life Church has largely grown because of a revitalizing experience of God's Holy Spirit. This has dramatically affected the way we worship. In our services, worshippers are free to respond to God in whatever way seems appropriate: to stand, sing, or just remain silent. One can

feel free to participate, or simply soak up the sense of God's presence. There is no compulsion or pressure apart from the prompting of God's Spirit.

And that's exactly the way it comes across. A seeking non-believer or unconvinced charismatic can feel as much at home as a hard core convert. In that sense it would be true to say that worship at NLC is missional. That is to say, all are invited to make God the focus in the worship; he then draws people irresistibly to himself.

With a variety of worship teams, including members with special gifting in instrumental or vocal musicianship, there is richness in the originality and diversity of the worship (Ps. 150:4; 134:2; Eph. 5:19). On occasion, the open worship time (not all pre-programmed from the front, although sensitively led) leads to words of prophecy or people coming forward for special prayer or confession. Worship and praise is unhurried in both the morning and evening services and is undoubtedly a source of attraction for those not yet experiencing God.

Not to be separated too rigidly from worship, prayer at NLC is a vital part of the corporate life. In 2004, a successful 24-hours-per-day week-long prayer chain on site in Jubilee Hall engaged almost two hundred different people in unbroken intercession. Displays were put up in the hall of the church's different ministries and people involved in them. Opportunity was given for participants to write thoughts that had come to them as they meditated and prayed in the designated areas. One could walk around from station to station to discover new facets of church life, scribble special prayer requests, listen to worship music, and pray-around-the-world. It was there that I grasped the true scope of NLC's ministry and decided that she warranted being featured in this book as a missional church.

Conclusion

Good things happen when churches are borderless. Lives are transformed, opportune witnessing encounters arise, and the most unlovable get saved when a church is not self-absorbed but looking to bless others. When you do not define yourself ecclesiastically by the four walls of the church edifice, blessing follows blessing, like winter flu making the rounds.

Let me illustrate. If NLC had not over the years built up a solid reputation in the community for her Christmas dinners for the lonely and marginalized of the community, the mayor of Worthing and his wife would not have dropped by on 25 December 2004 while the festivities were in full swing. And because the mayor's wife, a moderate Muslim, was there, she had the message of Christ shared with her in word and in deed. She got into conversation with my wife, possibly because of Linda's exotic accent and the mayor's wife having a relative in Toronto. She pointedly told Linda that she felt that all ways led to the same God. Linda then took the opening to politely but clearly state the opposite and share something of her faith story.

The world is your oyster if you are a borderless church.

9. The Uneasy Peace between Church and Parachurch

With such dynamic community involvement plus concerted global vision on the part of local churches, who needs parachurch organizations? Having served as the pastor of two churches over an eight-year span and also having spent 25 years in parachurch organizations, I have sat on both sides of the pastor's desk. In both roles, I felt slightly ill at ease as I related to my ministry counterpart. Like one might say about Mafia thugs, 'I know too much.' The church seems to be suffering from a schizophrenic personality. While she is rediscovering her missional calling, a very healthy development, the world of the parachurch continues to loom larger than life. One estimate is that there are one hundred thousand parachurch ministries in the US alone, most beginning since the end of the Second World War.[1] That there has been an uneasy peace between church and parachurch for a long time is well-known by the leaders of both parties, if not by the average person in the pews. It would be remiss not to address this issue in defending the concept of the borderless church. Even as I look at the last sentence, I think how ironic it is to be championing the emergence of the missional church when my very existence as a parachurch leader depends on convincing you that parachurch ministry is needed and valid!

But bad blood can exist between church and parachurch. Here's one true illustration: a mega-church in California told the organization that one of their missionaries was working with that his church had decided to discontinue the ministry of the missionary. 'We didn't approve of what the missionary was doing, so we told him that he and his family had to return to the States,' the elder declared. 'After all, he's supported by us 100 per cent. He's our missionary.'

'But doesn't he work for an agency?' was the rejoinder. 'Aren't they his employer and supervisor?'

'Yes,' said the elder, 'but we pay the bill; the agency doesn't.'[2]

Defining the parachurch

Few question the right of parachurch ministries to exist alongside the local church, even if the latter is usually understood to be God's primary method of expressing and extending his rule on earth. The former has existed since NT times, for example Paul's formation of an international team drawn from more than one church (Acts 20:4). Church historians are only too aware of ministries to spread the gospel functioning alongside, but separate from, the local church. When I first visited Northern Ireland for speaking engagements, I took the opportunity to visit the site of the first church planted there by Patrick in the 400s. The subsequent Celtic monastic movement, which was the primary medieval means of evangelizing Europe, is just one of the 'success' stories of parachurch structures down through history. Most markedly, the parachurch missionary movement began in earnest with William Carey's founding of an independent missionary society for India in 1792.

Ralph Winter, renowned American missiologist, calls this duality of roles in mission the *modality* and the *sodality* of the church.[3] The modality is the church; the sodality is a structure set up outside the parameters of the local church, whether that be the religious order mentioned above, or modern trans-denominational mission agencies, like my own, Arab World Ministries, which was begun in 1881 as Mission to the Kabyles and Other Races by three British gentlemen, George Pearce, Grattan Guinness, and Edward Glenney, connected only by a common vision to reach North African Muslims for Christ.

The term *parachurch* (a more commonly-used term than *sodality*), simply adds the Greek preposition, *para*, meaning *before*, *beside*, or *beyond*, to *church*, thus describing how the parachurch is not emanating directly from a specific church although being connected to the church in her universal sense (*parachurch* describes 'Christian' ministry and individual Christians who come from churches, not from other institutions, like Woolworth's!). Summarizing the essence of the parachurch organization, Bosch says, 'Basically, the societies [parachurch ministries] were all organized on the voluntary principle and dependent on their members' contribution of time, energy, and money.'[4] Similarly, *The Dictionary of Christianity in America* defines *parachurch* as 'voluntary, not-for-profit associations of Christians working outside denominational control to achieve some specific ministry or social service.'[5] An early study of the two structures for mission concluded that 'we must recognize every ministry structure other than a local congregation as a para-local church structure.'[6]

Theological issues

While it might be expected that there would be theological concerns over the biblical validity of parachurch movements, especially when bypassing the local church in their eagerness to fulfil their divine mandate, that is not entirely the case. Repeatedly, Acts 13 is proffered as proof that the local church does the calling and sending of the missionary into mission. However, a careful exegesis of the passage raises the question of who really does the sending. Picking up at verse 2, we read, 'While they [the prophets and teachers of the church at Antioch] were worshiping the Lord and fasting, the Holy Spirit said, "Set apart for me Barnabas and Saul for the work to which I have called them." So after they had fasted and prayed, they placed their hands on them and sent them off.'

True, verse 4 describes the church as *sending* the twosome into missionary work. But verse 2 indicates that it is the Holy Spirit who *calls* Paul and Barnabas, not the church. Furthermore, as if to stress that the calling is divine and not human, the tense of the verb is perfect and therefore translated as 'I have called them', suggesting that the will of God for Paul had already been made plain to him. The call came individually; yet the authority rested neither with the individual nor with the church, but with the Holy Spirit (cf. Gal. 1:1, where Paul reiterates that his call to mission engagement is divine, or Acts 9:15 where Paul's calling to the Gentiles is associated with his conversion). Every other player in this picture is but acting in obedience to the Holy Spirit, the leaders of the church in their laying on of hands (v.3) simply being a symbolic way of affirming what the Holy Spirit had already done in setting apart these two trail-blazers for pioneer missionary evangelism. As if to seal this understanding of what had happened so dramatically at Antioch, verse 4 summarizes the incident by concluding that 'the two of them' had been 'sent on their way by the Holy Spirit'.⁷Yet another argument for the primacy of church over parachurch as being biblically defensible is the fact that as early churches formed, they did not express allegiance back to the first sending church at Antioch: the churches at Colossae, Ephesus, and Corinth were complete in themselves.[8] Nor did the first missionaries put themselves under the full accountability of the initial 'releasing' church at Antioch. Missionary leader, Frank Severn, makes this same point.

> During his second missionary journey Paul encouraged the churches already planted and added new members to his missionary team. These new members came from the churches he started (Acts 16:1–3). It should be observed that neither Antioch nor Jerusalem determined who should join the Pauline team. Paul and his fellow workers decided. Accountabilities became diverse as new team members were added.[9]

Reporting back in order to encourage and stimulate further prayer, as Paul and Barnabas did to the church at Antioch, is quite different than being accountable to her for mission strategy and instruction.

In his inimitable way of finding the truth between two extremes, John Stott, in the 'Theological Preamble' to the Statement coming out of the second Consultation on World Evangelization at Pattaya, Thailand in 1980, concludes this about the church – parachurch impasse: 'Here then are the two extremes to be avoided. The tendency of the 'establishment' to control individual initiatives runs the risk of *quenching the Spirit*. The tendency of voluntary organizations to insist on independence runs the risk of *ignoring the Body*. It is the age-old tension between authority and freedom. To quench the Spirit and to ignore the Body are both serious sins.'[10]

While few church leaders would go so far as to deny the biblical justification for the parachurch, most would want to hold the parachurch to some kind of accountability or connection with the local church or denominational bodies. Articulating the theology of this perspective well is Guder: 'The church's nature as both one *and* catholic means that these structures must exist in a symbiotic relationship with local congregations and their denominational structures. The apostolic character of the church implies a variety of ways in which her mission is carried out, and thus a variety of structures that a missiological ecclesiology must address.'[11]

The current uneasy peace

The dynamic between parachurch and church might be compared to what happens in the back seat of the car when the family goes on its annual summer vacation. Early peace between older and younger siblings gradually breaks down and squabbles begin. Sometimes the fighting breaks out because the older child, used to getting all the attention when the younger one could barely talk, now has to vie for her parents' attention. The *church* might be compared to the older child and the *parachurch* to the younger sibling.[12] Would you not, if a church leader, be tempted to be jealous if you knew that giving to parachurch organizations overtook giving to churches in this last decade, the latest figures revealing that globally $100 billion is given to parachurch organizations, but only $94 billion to local churches?[13]

Within the US alone, closely paralleled by the track record found in other western world countries, the mushrooming parachurch industry has seen the birth of more organizations in the last four decades than in the previous one and a half centuries of the nation's history.[14] Agencies that spring to mind include the Billy

Graham Evangelistic Association and World Vision, or on the other side of the Atlantic, Tear Fund and Oasis.

Wait a minute! That's not the whole story though. A reverse trend has been observed, particularly a phenomenon of the last decade. It is a case of churches choosing to bypass parachurch agencies as they decide to be more than a caricature of a missional church, getting involved in mission and evangelism directly, without tapping into the resources of parachurch specialists. Brethren Assemblies globally have long practised local church autonomy in sending out missionaries, but new denominational players are doing much the same thing, such as the 'New Churches' in the UK.[15] Admittedly, in certain cases, technology more than theology has been a decisive factor here. Globalization has made local churches and their members more aware of needy situations cross-culturally, such as learning about the new Central Asian states that are using their fledgling freedom not to give freedom of choice about religion, but to give Muslim majorities the opportunity to crack down on opposition. The Internet enables one to discover the unreached nature of the 99 per cent Muslim Maldives in the Indian Ocean while booking an all-inclusive holiday on-line. A survey of 157 evangelical churches in the UK in 2001 conducted by Global Connections exposed the fact that 31 per cent had a direct link with a church in another country and 24 per cent had already started their own mission projects overseas.[16] Certainly, churches in the majority world do not think twice about massaging such relationships, as evidenced in the outlook of Thy Kingdom Come Church, described in Chapter 11.

This disengagement from parachurch mission organizations is sometimes called *disintermediation*. Disintermediation is occurring in North American churches too. The trend there, though, tends to be associated more with what have been labelled *mega-churches*. Astoundingly, half of the churchgoers in the US attend the top 12 per cent of the country's churches.[17] An illustration of a mega-church looking askance at too close a relationship with parachurch agencies is described in Chapter 6, in the Mars Hill story. There, church-to-church arrangements are viewed as the primary way to proceed in mission.

At the end of the day, though, many churches that began their mission involvement on their own are swinging back to an intermediate position. They are recognizing, among other things, that they are not as well-equipped to identify, train, send, pastor overseas, and handle a host of practical issues (for example, what sort of visa to get in the receptor country and how to economically transfer money across borders and various currencies) as they thought they were. Baker aptly sums up this compromise stance that is emerging: 'Congregations want to be involved, and the question is the degree to which they will bypass agencies and thereby overlook lessons gained from long travail and hard-won experience. Forward-looking agencies are seeking ways to position themselves as advisory resources to congregations inclined to move out on their own.'[18]

Mistakes of parachurch mission organizations

What has driven the churches away from delegating their primary mission involvement to the parachurch? For some, it has been a rediscovery of a more missional theology of church. For others, it was simply feeling distance from active involvement since the mission organization tended to take care of the church's missionaries sent to them 'from the cradle to the grave'. Here is a catalogue of criticisms by churches about parachurch mission organizations.

- They have an attitude of superiority, that they are the experts on cross-cultural ministry and we will get it wrong if we do it ourselves.
- They strip mine our churches of our best people and finances while claiming to have a high view of the church.
- They can be manipulative, their repeated use of the term *partnership* being really a euphemism for getting what they want from us, without giving anything substantive back.
- They are more focused on 'saving souls', which sometimes results in converts not being integrated into local churches.
- They are not interested in win-win relationships but win-win rhetoric.[19]
- They have taught us a deficient mission theology of 'some can give, some can go, but all can pray', thus forcing a dichotomy between 'goers' and 'senders', between 'professional missionaries' and 'the mobilization of the laity'.
- They are too task-driven and so do not care adequately for the people that we have sent as missionaries through them.[20]
- They keep raising the bar with respect to standards (for example, requiring psychological resiliency, theological training, and experience in the local church prior to going) so that mission becomes the privy of the professional and thus preventing mission from being within the reach of the average church member.[21]

Mistakes of churches in mission

If the churches have it right, why is the world so unevangelized after two millennia? Exactly, say the parachurch mission organizations, and that's why we exist, not because we have an aversion to the local church, but to augment their ministries since what they are doing is not enough. Let's consider, then, some of the critiquing of churches in mission by the parachurch.

- They are too inward-looking and self-serving; someone has to reach the lost!
- They are naive about the plethora of complex issues that are involved in cross-cultural ministry: pre-field and on-field support to weather the effects of culture shock, integration to the receptor culture, the challenges of team ministry when that is intercultural, and reverse culture shock when returning home; the real cost of doing ministry, including providing things like health care in countries where there is no adequate infrastructure for it and providing for retirement for career missionaries; the stresses and vagaries of support raising (because few churches will furnish their missionary with full support).
- They oversimplify the claim that mission agencies are top-heavy, thus necessitating heavy administrative charges which they claim they can avoid if they send the missionaries themselves. Cutting out the middleman ends up short-changing the missionary.
- They end up throwing all of their financial weight behind the support of nationals, hence reducing mission abroad to surrogacy, in the process ignoring all of the issues of dependency that have impeded the spread of the gospel far more than they realize.

- They have put too much stock in short-term mission and have therefore shown how illiterate they are about missiology and the difficulties of breakthroughs in the Muslim, Hindu, Sikh, and Buddhist worlds.
- They give endless responsibilities to capable people without giving them the requisite authority and therefore lose talented leaders to parachurch organizations by default.[22]
- They use faulty exegesis in charging members to give all of their tithes to the local church, claiming that the *storehouse* in 'bring the whole tithe into the storehouse' (Mal. 3:10) is the OT equivalent of the NT church.[23]
- In spite of the multicultural complexity of urban settings in the west, church members still lack sufficient cross-cultural savvy to avoid imposing unnecessary cultural baggage on emerging churches where they minister in a geographically and culturally-distant place.[24]

Creative solutions for brokering the peace

Global Connections in the UK is an umbrella agency that is trying to stimulate dialogue and constructive solutions to this impasse between church and parachurch where it exists. Some of the ideas listed below come out of their forums between church and parachurch leaders, like the 'Survive or Thrive' conference in September 2003 or the 'Global Interface' event a year later.

- Mission agencies can offer specialized services for churches that, for the most part, want to take full responsibility for sending out and supervising their own missionaries. Specialized help may include providing language study and first term of service cross-cultural orientation, something a church in Brighton might be ill-equipped to do for someone needing to learn Marathi in Mumbai to work among Hindus in this mega-city of India. Observes missiological journalist, Stan Guthrie: 'Most churches ... are willing to dance with their long-term agency partners, who know the ropes when it comes to cross-cultural ministry, obtaining visas, and the thousand and one details associated with missions.'[25] As mega-church Bethlehem Baptist missions' pastor verbalizes: 'I don't feel we have the time or expertise to do what a well-run agency can do.'[26]

- Mission resource services like Adopt-A-People or Association of Church Missions Committees can provide windows of insight and counsel for churches seeking to focus on one of the three thousand unreached people groups yet without a viable indigenous witness.

- Parachurch missions can offer 'real' service to local churches rather than lip service to the notion of partnership. An example of this is how AWM is equipping church members in how to understand Islam and then helping the church to build friendships with Muslims in the community. In Toronto, an umbrella organization of parachurch missions has started a programme called *BeFriend*, which equips local believers in cross-cultural ministry to the huge Hindu, Muslim, and Sikh population there. Another example would be for churches to send a church-planting team (or part of one) to work in conjunction with the mission agency, as AWM has done with a New Frontiers church in the UK and Calvary Chapel churches in the US. If local involvement in mission is viewed as part of normal discipleship training, as in Bramalea Baptist Church (see Chapter 10) and

Mars Hill Church, helping the laity in our churches develop cross-cultural skills and sensitivity locally is a practical service which agencies with the experts can provide. This service is all the more urgent and strategic when 40 per cent of our fifteen-year olds in church have made a decision to take the name of Jesus into another culture but fewer than 5 per cent ever follow through.[27] User-friendly seminars and learning experiences for Generation Y young people can also help overcome a general illiteracy about church history and mission.[28]

• Mission agencies can make sure their missionaries spend quality time with their sending church when on Home Ministry Assignment (furlough).[29] Missionaries need to develop listening skills with their sending churches in addition to their traditional 'show and tell' function. Coincidentally, mission agency leaders need to demonstrate an ability to listen to what pastors and missions' committees are really asking and wanting.

Perhaps parachurch mission agencies of the future will need to be more niche-focused instead of spread over the globe as some sort of multinational corporation, thus enabling churches to clearly discriminate among agency voices so as to discern who will provide the right service(s) for them.[30]

New realities should open church and parachurch to giving up prescribed roles. Networking of various players in world evangelization should be encouraged. Global, multi-lateral cooperative mission ventures where church and parachurch and new churches on mission frontiers are partnering in unforeseen ways of a generation ago must be facilitated.[31] An example of this sort of networking would be finding ways that the rapidly-growing church in Algeria could receive adequate leadership and theological training for its household churches in a milieu where Bible colleges or seminaries could not exist. Drawing together national church leaders, relevant parachurch agencies, Christian foundations to provide seed money, and churches in the west to provide trainers or financial assistance could expedite a resolution to what continues to be a dilemma even though good things are happening – even along the lines suggested here.

Conclusion

In the seeking of a peace that will endure between church and parachurch, the rediscovery of the church's missional essence will presuppose that the church has theological priority, but not exclusivity, in the fulfilling of the Great Commission and the Great Commandment. Hammett argues for this cogently when he states

> The servant-partnership model … combines a positive appreciation for the ministry of parachurch groups with an emphasis on the theological priority of the church. Parachurch groups are seen as partners, or helpers, raised up by God to aid the church, but possessing a status subordinate to that of the church. Thus, the parachurch group should defer to the church, honor the church [and] accept its ministry under authority of the church… Still, the relationship is a partnership in which each has something to offer the other.[32]

Ultimately, though, in light of some of the enduring challenges to world evangelization, as outlined, for instance, in the chapter on the 10/40 Window, church and parachurch must understand that they need each other. Only a win-win attitude will produce the kind of synergy that will result in greater fruitfulness for the Kingdom. There are some wonderful relationships that I have had the privilege of being in the middle of as churches and parachurch agencies have with Christ-like humility learned to esteem each other more highly than themselves and sought for the quality of partnership that furthers the joint calling to take the whole gospel to the whole world by the whole church. May that partnership continue to strengthen.

10. What the Borderless Church Looks Like: Bramalea Baptist Church, Canada

We had only attended the church once, having just settled into Brampton, a bed-sit community of Toronto, but within a week the pastor, Stu Silvester, who had phoned to ask if he could come by to say 'hello', dropped by. Little did we realize at the time that his visit was symbolic of the outward-looking and evangelistic zeal of a church that grew from six hundred or so people in the early 80s to one thousand five hundred by 2005. What is remarkable about this church that became our sending church for some years is that their growth has supported a massive building project, all the while expanding their community outreach and world mission thrust.

The world's first *glocal* pastor?

It is there on his business card. Seriously. Ivan Kostka, Glocal Discipleship Pastor. If you do not believe me, check it out at www.bramaleabaptist.org. Earnest in ensuring that people get the message that this church is all about wedding global and local understanding of what mission is really about, Bramalea Baptist Church (BBC) is not afraid to trail blaze in order to stay true to their view of Scripture on the subject. This calling card designation of a pastor as *glocal* is one of the hints that this is a missional church. One of their recent church family newsletters, *Let's Talk!* stated: 'At Bramalea Baptist we talk of mission as the overflow of our love for God empowering us to reach out to our neighbours near and far – "across the street, around the world."' We shall shortly come back to how this church combines home and foreign mission in an integrated approach to doing mission. But let's first look at another indication of the missionality of Bramalea.

A multicultural church

BBC has become a mirror of the ethnic makeup of the community. That is saying a lot. Brampton has the highest concentration of Sikhs in the Greater Toronto Area. Hindus and Muslims from South Asia similarly are found there in abundance. Ivan himself is from India – typical of hundreds of thousands of South Asians who migrated to this land of opportunity in the 1980s, when visa restrictions were not as stringent as they are now. South Asian and Afro-Caribbean Canadians make up two of the largest visible minority groups in the church. According to the 2001 Census of Canada, 43 per cent of Peel County in which the church is found is made up of those not born in Canada. Furthermore, 63 per cent of Peel's growth between 1996 and 2001 was due to immigration. The top ten countries of origin in Peel are: India, UK, Poland, Jamaica, Pakistan, Guyana, Trinidad, Tobago, Vietnam, and Hong Kong. All told, the pastoral staff told me that there are people of about 23 nationalities that are members of the church.

The senior pastor Ian Campbell cites the multicultural complexity of the church as being one of the major factors in his being persuaded to pastor this church from 2002:

'I had been part of a movement called 'Intentionally
Intercultural Churches' for the last couple of years and
it sounded like what I was passionate about, the church
was passionate about.'[1]

ICAN (Integration Centre for all Newcomers) is a
BBC ministry designed to attract visible minorities to
the church, especially those from unreached worlds. In
seeking to persuade a previously WASP[2] congregation
of the validity of ICAN, their church family newsletter
urges that 'our vision is to integrate not only visitors
to Bramalea Baptist Church into the life of the church,
but to reach out and touch the lives of new neighbors
with the love and truth of Christ.'[3] Perhaps aware of
some resistance to non-whites moving into the church
mainstream, the same newsletter empathetically argues
that 'it can be difficult enough to love and embrace our
brothers and sisters in Christ across generations and
cultures. But total non-Christian strangers? That is in
fact what the writer to the Hebrews exhorts us to do
right after "Keep on loving each other as brothers": Do
not forget to entertain strangers. For by so doing some
people have entertained angels without knowing it –
Hebrews 13:1–2, NIV).'[4]

ICAN on a practical level mobilizes the laity of
the church to offer rides to new immigrants to local
government offices so that people can register for things
as simple as universal health care services, donate
furniture (or help someone move), teach them English,
help them with job search skills like becoming computer-
literate, or simply befriend them through providing a
cup of tea or a simple meal.

The borderless nature of the church that ICAN
engenders is seen in this story. While visiting high rise
buildings nearby in which mainly new immigrants
were to be found, Ivan's wife Sylvia and a missionary

intentionally working with the church to reach out to new immigrants Candy Rosenberg discovered a group of new arrivals to Canada of only two weeks. Some agents had deceived the newly-arrived by promising them training so that they would be able to land jobs shortly after arriving in the country, meanwhile charging them exorbitant rents for their first month and stacking three families per apartment. These people were very upset, bitter, and hurt. Most were high caste Hindus, able to converse in English, and professionals back home.

The church was just starting new ICAN workshops at the time, ones in which training was given in job search skills, beginner's English classes, introduction to acquiring computer literacy, and introduction to Canadian culture. Right away the newcomers to Canada showed up for the classes to which Sylvia and Candy had invited them, and then the next day en masse to the morning service at church. Ian, from the front, made reference to them, welcoming them and invited people from the congregation to come alongside of them. Now that's the borderless church in action!

Illustrative of what ICAN has been doing to envision the church as a whole to be more multicultural in her outlook is the 2004 summer effort of ICAN and the Children's Ministry, which saw the two ministries joining hands to cross the street from the church building to a cluster of high rise apartment buildings known for their heavy concentration of new immigrants. After extensive advertising, a Kidz Klub was held in one of the apartment buildings themselves, offered in the mornings for three weeks. After some cross-cultural training for the staff, the team launched into a three-week programme: good moral character taught in week one using Galatians 5:22–23 as the text (46 kids from the surrounding buildings attended), continued low-key Bible-based instruction in week two while children enjoyed being 'In the Tropics' (50 children attended), and in week three the kids discussed 'Super Heroes' during one of the Olympic weeks as they heard of ancient biblical heroes, professional sports' figures, and giants of history (52 children attended). Participants included children from Afghanistan, Pakistan, Iran, Lebanon, and India. A final event saw parents invited. Among those attending were several Muslim mothers clad in their full black covering called a burka. Relationships continue with those who would not easily cross the street to the church building but who feel loved by those within the community and will send their children back for more ICAN events next summer.

Apart from reaching the unsaved and unchurched, one might still ask, what makes a multicultural church borderless or missional? The book of Acts suggests the answer: the proliferation of tongues spoken as the Holy Spirit fell upon the church in Jerusalem (chap. 2) became a sign that the gospel was not for Jews only, but had universal validity. That sign in contemporary church is no better demonstrated surely than by the presence of unity in the face of cultural diversity, that is, when a church is multiculturally vibrant. Concurring with this perspective is Guder when he postulates: 'The multicultural diversity of the church demonstrates that the gospel is going to the ends of the earth.'[5] In similar vein, Bramalea's senior pastor animatedly maintains: 'My view of the church that Christ is calling is an intercultural church and in the vision of Revelation is an intercultural church not by necessity but by delight, and I think that what God has been doing throughout salvation history is getting ready for that.'

It needs to be said that it is still quite rare for North American churches to be very multicultural when worship services are merged. What is a well-documented phenomenon is that the colour barrier is perceived to be broken when, for instance, a Somali congregation or an Egyptian and a Chinese congregation share facilities with a largely Caucasian church.

Here's a case in point. On a recent ministry trip to Toronto, which has a mammoth Chinese population, I counselled a Chinese couple who had started a Mandarin ministry in a Baptist church made up almost exclusively of Caucasians. Everyone was happy until the sheer numbers of Chinese coming to faith and attending the main service threatened to outnumber the mainstream population. Then the rumblings started about how 'we don't want to be taken over by people unlike us'. Scandalized at the repeated unchristian snubs, this dear brother and sister agonized about whether to leave the church and their racial prejudice or seek to reform from within.

Having intimated the problems with starting genuinely multicultural churches, such imbalance does not seem to be true of Bramalea. Something as simple as the leadership's preferred use of *intercultural* over *multicultural* to describe the cultural diversity of the church speaks volumes. Campbell intones, 'Since I have been here I have heard people talking more about being intercultural and I think it is important to use *inter* and not *multi* language in Canada because multicultural can just mean there are many cultures here, whereas intercultural begins to connote that these cultures have some interrelationships but are not just co-existent.' Truly this church has heeded the exhortation given to God's people millennia ago: 'Do not mistreat the stranger or oppress him for you were aliens in Egypt.' Non-Caucasians have been empowered and make up a significant percentage of the leadership within the church.

While estimates of Canada's evangelical composition range from 7 to 15 per cent, it has been calculated that approximately 5 per cent of the immigrant population is truly Christian.[6] Plenty of postmoderns there are to evangelize in the surrounding community, but the church's focus on new immigrants strategically means that they are reaching out to a group less evangelized than the mainstream population, surely a sign of missionality.

Can multiculturalism be taken too far? That is my own conviction – although it is becoming fashionable among evangelicals to push for all urban churches to become multicultural. The flaw of this perspective in my view is that emphasizing unity too much (laudable and biblical as the unity goal is – Eph. 4:11–6; Jn. 17), there is a potential levelling of cultural distinctives to some sort of globalized blob. But I suspect true unity is as much about achieving harmony while respecting and cherishing differences, not in seeking to minimize them, while retaining some veneer of diversity.[7] While a homogenous unit church can become so ingrown and self-absorbed that her unique worship language and cultural distinctiveness makes no room for the larger body of Christ, there is the need for people to feel at home where they worship in community. Especially true of first generational churches, whether among high caste Hindus in Sheffield or Muslim Background Believers (MBBs) in Lebanon, church plants that do not fit into the general Christian population make sense and have biblical precedent on their side (for instance, the first Gentile convert churches being allowed to be culturally non-Jewish – Acts 15). My own observation is that those coming from ancient civilizations, such as South Asians, Chinese, and Arabs, do not so easily integrate into heterogeneous churches, even after two or three generations in diaspora.

Notwithstanding this worry about overemphasis on multiculturalism in urban churches in the western world, my impression is that BBC has found a healthy balance in dealing with these extremes. While celebrating cultural diversity and its richness in the corporate worship services and in her general philosophy of ministry, Bramalea takes into account the need for those whose mother tongue is not English to fit into small groups where they can meet with their own type of people. Thus found at Bramalea, for instance, are Indian groups worshipping in Punjabi, Tamil, and Urdu, and one made up of Caribbean-Canadians. A concluding comment on the church's intentional intercultural makeup from Ian Campbell: 'It is all born out of a core missional heart that is all about reaching the lost.'

The centrality of the worship experience

As we have seen in other missional churches, worship plays an integral role in the unfolding of a God-centred emphasis that attracts the unchurched and edifies the churched. Bramalea's *Worship Arts Ministries* brochure states, 'We're convinced that all people are created for one primary purpose – to worship God. The reality is that all people worship, what they worship is another matter. We desire, as a congregation, to worship the Lord God Almighty, creator of heaven and earth, in spirit and in truth through Jesus, empowered by the Holy Spirit.'

Apart from intentional changes being introduced to the main Sunday morning services, Celebrate Recovery (a 12 Steps programme) devotes about 30 minutes to corporate worship and seeks to utilize various art forms in their worship experience as attendees move toward inner healing. Similarly, the many small groups in the church are encouraged not only to incorporate Bible study and fellowship into their gatherings, but an inspirational poem, a dramatic reading, or songs that will enable all to focus on the greatness and wonder of God. Sunday evenings, the Quarry, a youth worship service, meets to combine teaching and musical sounds to enable youth to connect with God in an experiential fashion. What is remarkable about the worship dimension of the church's ministry strategy, though, is this statement, which concludes the promotional brochure.

> As a ministering body, we're attempting to learn to *Speak the Language of the Person at the Door*. We recognize that many walk or are brought through our doors with little or no church background. They don't speak our language so we're determined to speak theirs well. We're constantly developing our abilities with the languages of the heart, the artistic expressions that transcend generational cultures, ethnic cultures and experiential cultures.

In other words, worship is viewed by the pastoral team as an evangelistic tool and is not limited to having value for believers. Unlike Mars Hill Church, BBC is crossing cultural barriers that are not so much postmodern as civilizational, that is, relating to other world religions and fundamentally different cultures.

As I met with them, the pastoral team latched onto an example of how worship at BBC is missional. They described how one of their most exciting and well-received worship services involved a fusion approach to music where they invited an outside Indian-style group with their sitar and tabla to merge with the regular worship team's guitars and style to produce a new sound. Indian bhajans (worship music) were blended into the service with western style worship music. Ivan enthused: 'It was like a holy wave swept across the congregation who were saying, "Oh, my goodness, that worship transcends two different forms of music and fuses it into something that is truly intercultural and truly spiritual."'

Seeking to appeal to the postmodern generation as well, the preaching is less traditional. The speaker may sit on a stool and essentially unwrap biblical truth through story-telling. Ian maintains: 'We try to have a lot more experience in a service as opposed to emphasizing the cerebral, and therefore we try to involve all of the senses in more intentional ways. We also see the whole service as a seamless entity. We see it as something to bring forward all kinds of artwork. We will have drama, live art, and whatever brings people into learning and changing.'

Michael Brandon, one of the church's longstanding members, reminds us that the church is not just intercultural but intergenerational. He speaks with a ring of authority, being both an elder and someone who has seen three pastors come and go, when he indicates that he misses some of the traditional hymns and quieter services but that 'it is exciting to see the unity being cultivated among many people from different cultures... I think there are still some areas that I am getting used to, such as I would rather have quietness to meditate rather than the noisy music, but then you see new Christians filled with joy the way things are presented so that you say, "Who am I?"'

Is this style of service resonating with attendees? A common response is something like 'I came here for three months and I could not stop crying [referring to sensing the Holy Spirit's presence].' People consistently stream to the front of the sanctuary at a service's end

for prayer. Something is resonating with the seekers who
throng to the church.

Small groups

The 'Vision Renewal Plan 2002–2007' brochure of BBC
describes her as a big and a small church. It is the small
groups that enable a church large by Canadian standards
to appeal to those who need to belong and experience
intimate relationships. Choosing from one of 300
small groups should do the trick! Strategically, BBC is
structured in three layers; the thousands, the hundreds,
and the tens. The ultimate goal of the three structures,
though, is very missional: 'BBC is committed to the
development of people for mission from the doorstep to
the end of the earth who know and use their spiritual
gifts in meaningful life and service', as the church's
welcome brochure declares.

The value the church places on small groups to provide
for people's growth, pastoral care, and developing of
enriching relationships is apparent in the way in which
elders are deployed. Each elder shepherds a cluster of small
groups. Instead of being the business or organizational
leaders of the church, the elders provide for spiritual
oversight and have relational responsibilities.

Having sat in on several of the small groups over the
years as my wife and I participated in BBC's annual
mission conferences, we have been impressed by the
familiarity and closeness which each group member
seems to have toward one another. Small groups help
the hugeness of the whole church to be digested. I
suspect that mega-churches cannot survive in the future
if they don't fathom the reality that new immigrants
and postmodern young adults cannot function easily or

comfortably without a small group, as we saw earlier with the protagonists of Coupland's satire, *Generation X*, a collection of a few people who hang out together, suspicious of the world at large, and who stick together through thick and thin. A missional church understands that 'no man is an island entire of itself' and so becomes seeker and new believer-friendly by making place for 'small is beautiful' feelings of those finding their place in the Body of Christ.

The size of the mission budget speaks volumes

While a missionary in India, I was told the true story of a Hindu convert being baptized in his white pyjamas, only to realize at the last moment as he was going under that he had left some rupee notes in his inside pocket, whereupon he fished them out and held them high in his clutched fingers as he otherwise went under the water. A good spiritual barometer of a church is how much of her budget will be set aside for overseas mission and local outreach. BBC does not disappoint in this regard. About one-third of her budget goes directly into mission. There you find the attitude evinced in Warren's bestseller: 'Money spent on evangelism is never an expense, it's always an investment.'[8]

Historically a church that saw mission as 'over there' and 'not here', BBC until recent years saw much of her budget and energy focused on sending and supporting foreign missionaries. They have not lost that level of fiscal commitment to overseas mission, given the watchful eye of passionate world Christians like Wayne Matthews, who coordinates *Perspectives on the World Christian Movement* courses conducted across Toronto. But a greater awareness of and involvement in addressing needs in the community has augmented the total mission strategy of BBC.

In their Wellness Ministries, for example, BBC has a Divorce Recovery group, a Just Me & the Kids programme for single parents and their children, Peace Work, which helps children learn how to manage conflict, and the Alpha programme. These ministries reach out both to church folk and to those who walk in off the street. For instance, Kathy, pastor of counselling, tells of a couple of Hindu ladies she has helped deal with inner wounds due to feeling disempowered by what their culture conveys to them about women being of little intrinsic worth and they have come to discover that Christ holds them in high esteem.

Commenting on this shift to a more balanced approach to mission, Mike, long-time member of the church, is convinced global involvement has not lost out, when he says,

> Mission is a continuum and it doesn't go just one way, so we see people coming and going all the time. We see people overseas more than before, but more for short-term. We have a back and forth sort of thing going on ... The most interesting question to ask of people in Toronto is "Where are you from?" No one takes offence because there is a delight in "Have you been to where I am from?" and if you have, all of a sudden you are my friend. I think our approach to global mission has brought a global consciousness to our church that is far more responsible than our previous association of mission being primarily about overseas work.

An example of the seamlessness with which the church goes about mission is the story of the Malabashs, originally from Trinidad. They have been involved with

BBC's Alpha programme from early on, then taking one of the 'graduating' Alpha groups into the Beta small group strategy, which has been sustained by them over a number of years. Peter Malabash has a brother in Trinidad who is an Anglican priest. Peter had this dream of taking Alpha to his brother's parish in Trinidad. After sharing this with Ivan Kostka, the church decided to provide some financial aid to Peter since the cost was too much for him alone. In 2004, Peter and his daughter went to Trinidad, and in three weeks were able to do leadership training and launch the first Alpha programme for three parishes. Ivan's response to this initiative welling up from within the congregation was:

> Increasingly, we want to see people involved in mission here, across the road, and around the world. Furthermore, that it is not about having done our bit in mission but, rather, now that we have come back, we want mission to be a part of our everyday world. So, for instance, with the youth as they go to the Dominican Republic year after year for short-term mission, our Youth Pastor Dean Kennedy has tried to say that everyone is on the team although not everyone goes. We are on mission all the time. Sometimes we just happen to go around the world and do mission somewhere else.

Ivan speaks about how Alpha has been instrumental in many unsaved becoming soundly converted and integrated into the church community. However, the church does not view mission as just being about conversion. What BBC is all about is making disciples of Christ. Therefore, Alpha streams into Beta, a 12-session discipleship course using Neil Anderson materials. Then comes the *Growing in Christ* inductive Bible study courses based on Precept materials, followed by *Serving Christ*, six sessions or one week-end spent in discovering one's spiritual gifts, personality type, and interest in service, followed by a course on learning how to share one's faith called *Sharing Christ*, and ending with *Operation Worldview*, a dynamic course, started by the US Center for World Missions, referred to earlier called *Perspectives on the World Christian Movement*. Other courses attend to the special needs involving men, marriage, financial stewardship, and boundaries in relationships.

In the promotional brochure advertising these growth opportunities, entitled *The Journey*, the vision of this discipleship focus is encapsulated in this statement: 'At BBC we facilitate [the on-going development of the whole person in Christ] with the "path of intentional discipleship". We call it The Journey.' Again, we see here an integrative approach to ministry, one which always includes space for the unbeliever to discover Christ, and therefore a philosophy of ministry that is missional.

Conclusion

As we hop from one lily pad to another while peering below the water's surface to see what makes missional churches appear, we are not so much attracted by answering the question of 'what makes churches grow' as we are by 'what distinguishes a borderless church from one trapped inside the walls of her building'. Three of the four churches we have devoted chapters to in this book are what could be described as mega-churches within their own societies, as Bramalea is. However, a missional church is not defined by her numerical size. As we have been seeing, there are certain attitudinal and functional features that distinguish missional churches from their Constantinian counterparts. Most of those features are part of the fabric of BBC.

At the end of the day, missionality is proved or disproved by the people who individually make up the church and are either missionaries in their outlook and praxis or not. As I met with the pastoral team, it did not escape my attention that the team was wracking their brains to put a human face on their own conviction that they were a borderless church. One that touched my heart was the story of one of their elders, a dentist who hailed from Myanmar. As it was recounted to me, this man was asked several years ago by one of his patients, a lady from the church, if he ever prayed for his patients. He replied that he had never thought of doing that. As a result of this exhortation, this brother began to pray out loud for his patients as they came to have their teeth tended to. He continues the practice to this day. A church that is borderless produces members like the dentist from Myanmar and the lady that held him accountable for being Christ's witness where God had placed him.

11. What the Borderless Church Looks Like: Thy Kingdom Come Church, Lostland[1]

In spite of being from the world's largest and most universal religion, Christians are still treated with hostility to varying degrees, including outright persecution, in vast swathes of Asia, Africa, and elsewhere. Religions or ideologies, where they are in a majority, have a history of being intolerant toward Christians if we are talking about Islam, Hinduism, Buddhism, or communism. The borderless church delineated in this chapter inhabits such a world. Her story reveals that the missional church can take root in the soil of any culture or country.

I first visited Thy Kingdom Come Church (TKCC) in 2003 as the result of an invitation to their annual mission conference. To those convinced of the notion that mission conferences are a western world invention, they need to visit TKCC. In Lostland, the nation where this church is situated, 93 per cent of the population follow a god who is not the God of the Bible. In Lostland, conversion is illegal – unless you convert to the majority religion, that is. That this church has a mission conference is little short of a miracle.

Built in the 1940s, TKCC is one of those larger-than-life churches that grace the downtown core of world-class cities, close to tourist attractions and important historical or state buildings. Even in TKCC's early days, the property on which a sanctuary was subsequently erected was expensive to purchase, but God blessed the ministry with an anointed preacher, and with crowds flocking to hear him, much as they thronged to hear Charles Spurgeon decades earlier on another continent, his congregants found ways to purchase the land that he envisaged as being strategic for the advance of God's kingdom in Lostland.

For some church attendees, funding the property purchase meant melting the gold from their earrings. People of influence sought approval from the royal family to go ahead with the land purchase. Miraculously the permission was granted (one thinks of Nehemiah going before King Artaxerxes to get permission to go back to Jerusalem to rebuild the city walls in Neh. 2). In due course, an edifice seating 1300 people was built.[2]

After the death of the founder, attendance declined from an average of 800 to as low as 50 people, not at all helped by the fact that the church was located in a non-residential area. A new pastor, whom we shall call Pastor James, had a great passion for evangelism, even amongst those whom it was forbidden to proselytize. Among his strengths, ones we have seen evident in other missional churches, were leadership mentoring and being exercised in prayer.

There was a sense of expectancy in the late 70s and early 80s that the Lord was going to do something great. Revival broke out, especially amongst the young people. Prayer would continue for hours on end, with visions and worship, as people were riveted to their seats. Within several years, the college and career group grew to 500 attendees, unheard of in Lostland.

Those lean years disappeared to the degree that today there are six to seven thousand people associated with TKCC. From those years of growth pains, this church, flourishing like a palm tree in a desert oasis, has spawned ministries that are pre-evangelistic to the majority community through such culture-friendly ministries as running sports clinics and working with drug addicts.

Meanwhile, the first missionary went out from the church in 1988. Cross-cultural ministry started through short-term involvement and the influence of organizations like YWAM and OM – which gave structured opportunities to try mission out. At about the same time, the current associate pastor, whom we shall call Barnabas, was given a more visible leadership role, a fruit of the mentoring style of Pastor James' leadership. With Barnabas being a younger leader, this was an inspiration to the huge number of young people in TKCC. Pastor Paul attributes a discipling and mentoring modelling by the leaders for much of the church's success: 'We as leaders learned that we could not lead alone. This is how our growth in numbers came about. People could get discipled and were given opportunities to develop different ministries.'

Outreach to village areas in Lostland began. This was aimed at the nominal Christian community in the country. Evangelistic meetings were held in village churches that had closed their doors. Not only would nominal Christians be saved and revived, but the majority community would start attending meetings, bringing the sick and demon possessed. Repeat visits to responsive villages enabled discipleship and outreach training to start. By the mid-nineties a network of some three hundred and fifty churches had been formed, all through the instrumentality of TKCC.

More recently, this network has been used to bring over one thousand leaders from across Lostland to benefit from in-depth leadership equipping.

Intentional mission

In a restricted access country, sending missionaries across geographical boundaries is one of the cutting edge advances in mission of the twenty-first century. The Back to Jerusalem Movement of China talks in terms of 100,000 missionaries moving along the ancient Silk Road to evangelize unreached peoples across Central Asia and the Middle East. A few have been sent already. Even if only a few thousand actually go, that contribution from the east will be a significant accomplishment. In spite of the Hindu hegemony in India, parachurch organizations like India Evangelical Mission and OM-India send out nationals to neighbouring Hindu, Muslim, Sikh, or Buddhist countries. TKCC is part of this trend of mission from everywhere to everywhere. At present, 35 adults have been sent out into mission by this church alone (not just adopted, but having TKCC as the church in which they grew up).

Sharing his own testimony about getting involved in mission, the mission pastor, Paul, related to me the following.

> 1983 was the first time I travelled out of Lostland. Before that I saw some western missionaries ... living in Lostland and this was inspiring, encouraging. These people were crossing over cultural [and linguistic] barriers. When I went to [a nearby country] and heard about how much they wanted [our people] to come to help them because we knew the language ... I felt excited ... I ended up in Los Angeles in front of the football stadium giving Bibles to [people from a very restricted country] and this was the first time I gave a Bible to [someone of the majority religion found in my own country]. This short-term trip made the vision [of mission] more and more clear for me personally. My church ... felt

we should continue [to send people into the world where we knew the language already] and so this ministry was developed little by little ...

We started in 1988 by sending one person out, and then in 1990 we had outreaches from our church in five countries, and then in 1992 we started having more long-term people [getting involved]. Then we went to Barcelona to work among [our own type of people] there. It was usually done by sending someone via another mission agency ... Growing little by little, with more and more people going to the field, we felt that we should have a mission board ... All the salaries and mission work expenses [came initially] from the church offerings ... We have eight congregations [so we can spread the financial burden around somewhat]. Now the mission budget is greater than the church budget. For the mission work the funds range from 25–35 per cent coming from the church and the rest is mainly western funds ...

About ten adults are working within Lostland and 25 outside of Lostland. They all work in countries where the same language they know can be used. We know the language so we can fit in from day one. There is no culture shock. [Nevertheless because of the geographical and religious difference] it is still a cross-cultural experience. Long-term workers must learn the dialect and subculture of the area. We still have lessons to learn but we do have a big advantage [over non-native Lostland speakers].

Merging the local and the global

You may have noticed that Pastor Paul indicated that (in spite of the restrictions on open witness to those of other faiths within Lostland) about one-third of their missionaries were ministering within Lostland. Such a commitment is courageous given the possible consequences in Lostland if one is found witnessing to people of the majority religion. This 'being wise as serpents but harmless as doves' approach stems in no small part from Pastor Barnabas' unswerving resolve to engage in careful witness in the face of relentless psychological pressure, or so Pastor Barnabas is convinced.

People in the church were arrested in the early 1990s because of their failure to kowtow to the status quo of being inward-looking churches. Pastor Barnabas was threatened with death and interrogated intermittently. He often related to the church how prayer got him out of situations where he found himself between a rock and a hard place with the authorities. He was a good teacher on apologetics and some of his students started doing seminars all over Lostland multiplying the fruit of his passion for the majority population. Not only did this give people confidence to step out of their comfort zone but it introduced them to those from the majority faith who were open to the gospel and who, in some cases, were seeing Jesus in dreams and visions. It was as if they were waiting for Stephen to come along to the Ethiopian eunuch to explain the meaning of what he was reading about the Messiah.

Perhaps the most outstanding ministry engaged in by the church within Lostland is her drug rehabilitation centre, located in the countryside and run by a dedicated staff. While visiting the site in 2003, I met those whose lives had been transformed by the caring community. All four churches highlighted in this book see ministering to the physical and emotional needs of people in their communities or on the other side of the globe as inextricably linked to gospel witness. They would concur with Stevens' eloquent words: 'Common salt is composed of two deadly poisons, sodium and chloride. Taken separately in sufficient quantity they will destroy life. Together they are essential for life. The church's mission is composed of *both* evangelism and social action and each is deadly without the other. In *this* way we are the salt of the earth.'[3]

Déjà vu with the small group core value

As we have seen repeatedly with borderless churches, small or cell groups feature in the way 'church' is conceptualized. As early as 1993, the TKCC church leadership decided that each church member should be in a small group. The whole church is divided into eight congregations for meetings and services. The pattern of ministry through programmes is the same for each congregation, whether we are talking about morning and evening Sunday services or college and careers groups. Each congregation has her own evangelism team, worship team, etc. The leaders of each group form the senior leaders of the pastoral team of the church. Each age group is subdivided into cell groups. It is expected that cell groups will grow and expand by meiosis. This happens as friends are invited by cell members into the group. Hence the cell groups also have an evangelistic edge to them. Parallel to this are the discipleship classes, a reminder of how Bramalea Baptist integrates small groups into their missional outlook.

Mission exists because worship does not

A fitting illustration of this insightful Piper theme of mission needing to continue simply because there are peoples within which the true and living God is not worshipped is the way that one is struck by the presence of God in a majority world church where the God of the Bible is brilliantly worshipped. As I attended the mission conference of TKCC in 2003, I was struck by the sensitive and passionate worship of the worship teams and the church members. Some of the worship was in the local language and some in English but there was no mistaking the presence of the Holy Spirit. This we have repeatedly seen to be a common feature of borderless churches, so why should we be surprised that there was no spiritual desert in TKCC, Lostland? When God's people have their eyes lifted away from themselves to the living God, they become missional (Is.6:1–9).

Similarly, the spirit of prayer pervades the meetings, not that one should be surprised when correlating the history of the church and the advance of mission, such as demonstrated by the Moravians. Pastor Paul echoes this strain of prayer and worship running through TKCC's DNA when he confides: 'Our leaders say that it is a very dangerous thing not to pray because it means that you depend on yourself. Prayer in itself is an act of trust in God. What we are asking [in terms of their mission vision] is too great for anyone to take on and that is why we need to pray. Five years ago we started a new way of prayer and had a prayer conference which attracted over four thousand people. It developed into a prayer network not just for our church only coming to pray for ourselves but learning to pray for Lostland and the wider region.' Here we see prayer inexorably linked to mission. The two go together like England and fish and chips. This correlation between prayer and missionality has been observed already in our study, such as with New Life Church. It is a pattern discerned in a recent study of American churches thought to be demonstrating their borderless nature.[4]

Willingness to suffer for faith is also missional

We saw in Chapter 4 how the early church grew as she withstood the persecution unleashed on her. Of the four churches considered in depth in this book, only TKCC operates from the margins of society. The others still benefit from the traces of Christendom embedded in the cultures within which they are seeking to be borderless. The Cross is not a symbol to be exhibited larger than life facing the street traffic at a major intersection, as it is for Bramalea Baptist, but synonymous with suffering, as it is for TKCC. We have already noted that the NT word for 'witness' is *martyria*. Early church father, Tertullian, not without reason, observed that 'the blood of the martyrs is the seed of the church'. TKCC cautiously but unflinchingly accepts that to be missional means to take calculated risks and to function in harm's way. Little wonder that this is a Thessalonian-like church whose courageous faith is known locally and globally. When you want to put a face on the borderless church of the future, think Thy Kingdom Come Church.

12. The Church's Mission is Not about Bricks and Mortar

It all starts with Jesus. Whether we are talking about the individual or the church. We are to shape our personal and corporate life after his example (1 Jn. 2:6). Collectively and individually we are his disciples. Without looking very far, we know that he built his life around satisfying the needs of others, not his own: 'For even the Son of Man did not come to be served, but to serve, and to give his life as a ransom for many' (Mk. 10:45). Similarly, a church that is acknowledging Christ as her head, as indeed he is (Eph. 4:15), will be borderless. She will see herself not in terms of bricks and mortar, but in terms of mission. Congregations will see buildings to meet in not only as nice – but as a means to the end of reaching out, into the community and around the world. They will distinguish between a church and a community of Christians as surely as they will between a building and a pile of stones.[1]

If everything is mission, is nothing mission?

'If everything is mission, nothing is mission' is a challenge broached by missionary statesman Stephen Neill decades ago, but which is an appropriate one to ask again, given the thrust of this book. It is a question instinctively asked in Christendom when the church is centre stage, and more concerned about maintaining her membership than catering for those beyond the pale. However, in seeing God's mission as giving the church her core meaning (in Chapter 1), the cart is no longer put before the horse. Whatever does not contribute to the church's being, doing, and telling of Christ as Saviour and Lord is not part of the church's calling.[2] As the pastor of one borderless church exclaims: 'Churches that are missional do not do missions as a program. Missional churches have moved from missions as doing to missions as being. In truly missional churches, the job of missions belongs to the whole body, rather than an elite group of people called missionaries. To be a disciple of Christ means that his mission to the nations is your mission.'[3]

Shaping the borderless church in the twenty-first century

With the church slipping to the margins of society in the west, facing globalization with its relativizing reinforcement of postmodernity, and finding herself in an increasingly religiously plural society where she is physically positioned, the twenty-first century presents her with an opportunity to start all over again. We have been determining what the shape of the borderless church might look like, both theoretically and practically. Here is a synthesis of all that specific missional churches, the community context, the example of the early church, and the sweep of Scripture has pointed us toward.

Start not with your core but with the community[4]

Bramalea Baptist designs her worship, her small group ministry, and her philosophy of ministry around the fact of the multicultural community surrounding her site; Mars Hill Church is driven by reshaping church for the postmodern unchurched and disillusioned post-Christians around her; New Life Church attracts and has designed her programmes for the elderly, the new immigrant, young families, and the marginalized in her community; Thy Kingdom Come Church is relentlessly pushing the boundaries of witness to the majority population with its different faith. These churches are all excited with God – not only because of who he is, but because of how he is using them to reclaim the broken and bruised of the world.

Start not with your core but with your community

Do not short-change worship

Churches attuned to their missional calling look beyond the comfort zones of long-time Christians to shape their worship. Disillusioned former church-goers and the pagan unchurched 'lament banal, uninspiring, repetitive, culturally dated forms of corporate worship, unrelated to life beyond the congregation'.[5] I have yet to find a church borderless in outlook that has not revitalized her worship and put the adoration of the Lord at the centre of congregational life. None of the four featured here is short-changing those who show up Sunday morning; attendees leave knowing that they have met with God. Filled with the joy of the Lord, these radiant saints will offer a kind response to the cynical remark of the engineer in the next work station on Monday. They will make the time to take the seriously disabled neighbour for walks by the seaside. They will leave a lucrative career as a medical doctor to learn a language and run a clinic for many years in Muslim Tajikistan. Tellingly, Newbigin declares: 'Mission is an acted out doxology. That is its deepest secret. Its purpose is that God may be glorified.'[6] Looked at holistically, of course, glorifying God not only occurs when we sing his praises but as we live all of life to his glory – and that is a fragrant aroma to those who are seeking after God (2 Cor. 2:15).

See that a sense of belonging is cultivated in intentional community

The power of small groups in engendering a sense of belonging – whether in church or in society – has been underscored repeatedly in this book. Whether we are talking about home groups making mega-churches palatable or deliberately working from a cell or house church strategy, vibrant community is a key component of borderless churches. One of the leaders of the Vineyard Movement talks about this type of church planting being in the genetic code of their churches: 'In the organizational culture where high value is placed on small group experiences, a new believer may lead someone else to the Lord, lead their own small group within a year, be mentoring an apprentice leader and already be dreaming of the day that they can help plant a church. More Generation Xers want to be planters, many of them overseas.'[7]

Only now being chronicled as the way churches multiply in the majority world, and which shows promise for penetrating the baked soil of parts of Asia, the Middle East, and North Africa, is a church planting movement through house churches.[8] Murray speaks of that phenomenon in the west: 'Some emerging churches are *reconfiguring community*. In fragmented, individualistic postmodernity, many long for authentic community and friendship. Churches at their best offer rich experiences of community – some homogenous, others spanning classes, generations, ethnicity and personalities – few groups can match this.'[9] Moreover, as we have seen in the way some home/small groups multiply in the four churches, 'in mission-oriented churches [friendship fostered in small groups] is inclusive, not exclusive, so people can belong before they believe.'[10]

Cultivate soft apologetics without going soft on the gospel

Engaging twenty-first century culture will require learning how to dance. It may seem awkward and strange at first, as it did for my wife and I taking dance lessons shortly after beginning to pastor that Chinese church in Toronto, where dancing was so much in the fabric of their wedding culture (one year I conducted six weddings!). In dancing, it has been observed, both partners have to adjust to each other, and like getting to know strangers in our neighbourhood or around the world, both partners have 'to build an authentic partnership [that] takes time and persistence ... an attitude of humility that allows for the graciousness of relationships to develop. It [requires] the opposite of moving into a situation or a relationship having all of the answers.'[11] Resistance to our message is out there, whether out of experience with evangelicals or formed by the media. Even in so-called evangelical America, non-Christians think more highly of soldiers, lawyers, and lesbians than they do of Christians.[12] Of necessity, evangelism is being retooled from 'exhortation and invitation' to 'incarnation and explanation'.[13]

At the same time, making our defence of the gospel less confrontational and anchored around being relational, our church programmes need to be soft toward those eager to build friendships with unsaved work colleagues or fellow students. Church programmes that do not lead to results among the unchurched or to equipping members to share their faith in the workplace or to discovering their spiritual gifts will need rationalizing.[14] Concomitantly, winning a hearing may take time but will lead, at the end of the day, to clear witness being given to the fact that 'Jesus is Lord'. Borderless churches can integrate into the community seamlessly and equip some to take on the hard places of the 10/40 Window by teaching a soft apologetics but not a soft gospel.

Foster a glocal church

Like the lady of justice blindfolded so as to dispense justice with impartiality, borderless churches will even-handedly engage the world beyond her doorsteps, across the street, and around the world. We can no longer afford the luxury of 'the thinking of many [which] is still governed by a ... linear model of mission, where it is all about the transmission of something *from* here *to* there.'[15] All four churches we focused on were freed from dated concepts of mission that enabled them objectively to assess where they had a special stewardship in ushering in God's kingdom. It inevitably led them to a healthy tension of urging their people to respond to local and global needs simultaneously. Summing up well the concept of the glocal, *ergo*, borderless church, missiologist George posits that 'the primary missionary agency today is a local congregation somewhere that is related

to the global church. All mission is two-way, sending
and receiving. Every congregation simultaneously is
sent to participate in God's transforming mission both
globally and locally ... In this new model, geographical
dichotomies and one-way mission belong to the
past.'[16]

Think and act holistically

Particularly in glimpsing the inner life of the Thessalonian
church and Thy Kingdom Come Church, we were
confronted with the need to think seamlessly about
the church's inner and outer worlds. Both churches
were renowned for their willingness to suffer for their
faith, not only in order to witness faithfully in word to
a hostile culture but in order to remain true to creed
and conduct. Disciple-making breeds Christ-likeness.
Christ-likeness is sure to attract persecution as much as
bees are drawn to nectar (Jn. 15:17–21). The moral state
of the church in the west undermines her ability to be
missional. Harris seizes on this in her passionate words:
'The danger of secularism is not so much what it does
to nonbelievers, it is what it does to the church. It erodes
our moral authority. It erodes our spiritual power, the
only true power.'[17] As civilizations increasingly clash,
in which religion pays a major role, as opposed to the
clash between nation-states, we can expect a polarization
of opinion about and hardening of attitude toward
any form of religious conservatism.[18] In such a milieu,
borderless church will bear witness in life more than
lip – much as the MBB underground churches of today
and the early churches of yesteryear. Missional churches
have discovered the need for radical discipleship, as
a recent survey of American churches thought to be

missional, has discerned. Articulating what was found in these churches, we are told that 'they are developing, sometimes painfully, skills in self-analysis and self-criticism, which move them close to what the Bible calls repentance. They are aware that change is hard, often painful, but unavoidable if Jesus is the one who is forming them. Their conviction is becoming more and more articulate that their formation as witnesses to God's reign is the reality that defines them.'[19] For such churches, the cross-bearing of genuine discipleship is not avoided, and sometimes that means persecution, for discipleship will inevitably involve extending the kingdom of God to those outside that kingdom.

But there is another dimension of holistic church that that will characterize the church of the new millennium. That will be the systemic uniting of word and deed in the community where the church is found and in her global commitments. Whether involving advocacy for the voiceless as Mars Hill Church does or practically assisting new immigrants as Bramalea Baptist does, such demonstration alongside proclamation is missional. Issues of the environment, religious liberty, and alleviation of urban poverty cannot be made second-class citizens of global witness. To cite one example of how this prophetic witness might play out, Ramachandra does not mince words: 'For Christians to practise this counter-narrative of globalization would involve a break with the nationalistic allegiances that have come to define us, along with others, in our respective nation-states. It would mean, for instance, British Christians openly identifying with their brethren in Burma and so challenging the commercial dealings of British companies with the Burmese military regime.'[20] The total life of the church community is what counts in true mission.[21]

Shape a new kind of leader

We face a paradox as we enter the twenty-first century. The challenges of globalization, post-Christendom, religious pluralism, civilization wars, and postmodernity plead for apostolic leaders in the church, not small-minded or inward-looking ones. Prophetically, McNeal contends: 'Many of today's Christian leaders, faced with similar challenges to those of the first apostles, will draw on leadership practices and principles of the initial leaders of the Christian movement.'[22] They will be servant leaders, facilitating their own people into doing the ministry and thus equipping them to face a desperate and decaying culture with confidence and faith; they will be missional, not concerned with preserving the status quo so much as being kingdom-minded, facing outward not inward, being luminous; they will guard and cultivate their own spiritual formation so that others are inspired and drawn to the God they follow; they will preach a message captured in this quote: 'Local churches cannot be ends in themselves, for the Church is not the final goal of mission. Local churches are, rather, the instruments of something much greater than themselves: They are the tools of the kingdom of God.'[23]

The hedgehog versus the fox

Part of our inherited wisdom comes in the form of an ancient Greek parable about the hedgehog and the fox. The fox is an intelligent creature, able to scheme and plan a variety of cunning attacks against the hedgehog. The fox circles around the hedgehog's den, day after day, poised to attack. Looking at the beautiful and swift animal, who would doubt the fox's ability to win out over the awkward-looking, cumbersome and ugly hedgehog, seemingly oblivious to impending attacks.

Not quite caught by surprise, though, the hedgehog succeeds in rolling up into a ball as the fox sneaks out of the blue upon its prey. The hedgehog immediately becomes a ball of sharp spikes pointed out in every direction, as if having a bad hair day. Foiled again, the fox retreats to the woods to develop a new strategy of assault. Each day, despite the superior cunning of the fox, the hedgehog comes out alive.[24]

Churches, correspondingly, are hedgehogs or foxes. Fox-like churches see their ministry and the world in all their complexity. They take their significance from maintaining a diversity of programmes and moving in many directions at once. They are wrapped up in surviving in a complicated world and so are programme-oriented rather than purposeful. Keeping it simple means to do everything on the basis of 'does it lead us to fulfil our purpose for existence: to bring glory to God by bringing the lost to Christ?' That is what hedgehog churches do: they may not have the most cutting edge Sunday school curriculum or necessarily a multi-person staff catering to every age group in the congregation, but hedgehog churches reduce complexity to a single organizing idea, to a guiding principle that unifies everything. Borderless churches have discovered the hedgehog principle. They are shedding everything that does not fit into their hedgehog idea that their purpose is missional. These are the churches that will win the hearts and minds of the world they inhabit in the twenty-first century, and it will be not only because they have brought order out of chaos but because they have rediscovered the right single idea of church.

Scripture Index

Subject Index

Bibliography

AD2000 Movement. *10/40 Window: Getting to the Core* (Colorado Springs, CO: AD2000 & Beyond Movement, 1999)

Adelphi, G. and E. Hahn, *The Integrity of the Bible according to the Qur'an and the Hadith* (Hyderabad: Henry Martyn Institute of Islamic Studies, 1977)

Adeney, M., 'Is God Colorblind or Colorful?' in R. Tiplady (ed.), *One World or Many?* (Pasadena, CA: William Carey, 2003), 87–104

Aganon, R., 'An International Family Affair', *Focus on the Family* (March 2000), 10

Amiel, B., 'Is France on the Way To Becoming an Islamic State?' *National Post* (21 January 2004)

Bailey, R.P., 'Who's Turning the Mission Field Upside Down', *Evangelical Missions Quarterly* (January 2001), 50–57

Baker, D.B., 'William Carey and the Business Model for Mission' in J.J. Bonk (ed.), *Between Past and Future* (Pasadena, CA: William Carey, 2003), 167–202

Barrett, D.B., and T.M. Johnson, 'Annual Statistical Table on Global Mission: 2004', *International Bulletin of Missionary Research* (January 2004), 24–5

Barrett, L.Y. et al., *Treasure in Clay Jars: Patterns in Missional Faithfulness* (Cambridge, UK: W.B. Eerdmans, 2004)

Beckham, B., 'The Church with Two Wings' in M. Green (ed.), *Church Without Walls* (Carlisle: Paternoster, 2002), 26–39

Bietenhard, H., 'People, Nations, Gentiles, Crowd, City' in C. Brown (ed.), *The New International Dictionary of New Testament Theology*, *Vol. 2* (Grand Rapids, MI: Zondervan, 1976), 788–805

Bjork, D.J., 'Foreign Missions: Next Door and Down the Street', *Christianity Today* (12 July 1985), 17–20

—, 'Toward a Trinitarian Understanding of Mission in Post-Christendom Lands', *Missiology: An International Review* (April 1999), 231–44

Bonhoeffer, D., *Letters and Papers from Prison* (London: Fontana, 1965)

Bonk, J.J., 'Thinking Small: Global Missions and American Churches', *Missiology: An International Review* (April 2000), 149–61

— (ed.), *Between Past and Future: Evangelical Mission Entering the Twenty-First Century* (Pasadena, CA: William Carey, 2003)

Borthwick, P., 'Mobilizing the Next Generation', *Evangelical Missions Quarterly* (October 2003), 434–442

Bosch, D.J., *Transforming Mission: Paradigm Shifts in Theology of Mission* (Maryknoll, NY: Orbis, 1996)

Bramalea Baptist Church, *Let's Talk*, (26 September 2003), 1–4

Bremner, C., 'Stoned to Death… Why Europe Is Starting to Lose its Faith in Islam', *The Times* (4 December 2004), 56

Brown, C. (ed.), *The New International Dictionary of New Testament Theology, Vol. 2* (Grand Rapids, MI: Zondervan, 1976)

Browne, B., 'Churches Revived by Multiculturalism', *Faith Today* (July/August 2001), 28–30

C., Joseph and Michele, 'Field-Governed Mission Structures: In the New Testament', *International Journal of Frontier Missions* (Summer 2001), 59–64

Callahan, K.L., *Effective Church Leadership: Building on the Twelve Keys* (San Francisco, CA: HarperSanFrancisco, 1994)

Camp, B.K., 'A Survey of the Local Church's Involvement in Global/Local Outreach' in J.J. Bonk (ed.), *Between Past and Future* (Pasadena, CA: William Carey, 2003), 203–47

Carson, D.A., *Biblical Interpretation and the Church: Text and Context* (Carlisle: Paternoster, 1993)

—, *The Gagging of God: Christianity Confronts Pluralism* (Grand Rapids, MI: Zondervan, 1996)

Clapp, R., *A Peculiar People: The Church as Culture in a Post-Christian Society* (Downer's Grove, IL: InterVarsity, 1996)

Clendenin, D.B., *Many Gods, Many Lords* (Grand Rapids, MI: Baker, 1995)

Clowney, E.P., 'Interpreting the Biblical Models of the Church' in D.A. Carson (ed.), *Biblical Interpretation and the Church* (Carlisle: Paternoster, 1993), 64–109

Collins, J., *Good to Great* (New York, NY: HarperCollins, 2001)

Colson, C., *The Body: Being Light in Darkness* (Milton Keynes: Word, 1992)

—, 'Salad-Bar Christianity', *Christianity Today* (7 August 2000), 80

Coupland, D., *Generation X* (London: Abacus, 1992)

Couto, J., 'Multicultural Diversity Growing in Canadian Churches', *ChristianWeek* (1 May 2001), 3–4

—, 'Reaching Immigrants from South Asia', *Faith Today* (January/February 2002), 44–6

Craig, W.L., 'Politically Incorrect Salvation' in T.R. Phillips and D.L. Okholm (eds.), *Christian Apologetics* (Downer's Grove, IL: InterVarsity, 1995), 76–97

Dawn, M.J., *Reaching Out Without Dumbing Down: A Theology of Worship for the Turn-of-the-Century Culture* (Grand Rapids, MI W.B. Eerdmans, 1995)

Douglas, I., 'Globalization and the Local Church' in M. Stackhouse (ed.), *The Local Church in a Global Era* (Cambridge: W.B. Eerdmans, 2000), 202–8

Dylhoff, J., 'Generation X', *Evangelical Missions Quarterly* (October 2003), 444–50

Erickson, M.R., *Truth or Consequences: The Promise and Perils of Postmodernism* (Downer's Grove, IL: InterVarsity, 2001)

Fernando, A., *The Christian's Attitude toward World Religions* (Wheaton, IL: Tyndale, 1995)

Foster, S., 'The Impatience of the Mission Agency with the Local Church', (Toronto: Lausanne Forum # 3, 2000)

Fouch, S., 'Globalization and Health Care Missions' in R. Tiplady (ed.), *One World or Many?* (Pasadena, CA: William Carey, 2003), 123–41

Friedman, T.L., *The Lexus and the Olive Tree* (New York, NY: Anchor, 2000)

Fuder, J., 'Training Students to Exegete the City', *Occasional Bulletin Evangelical Missiological Society* (Spring 2003), 4–6

Galadima, B., 'Religion and the Future of Christianity in the Global Village' in R. Tiplady (ed.), *One World or Many?* (Pasadena, CA: William Carey, 2003), 191–202

Garrison, D., *Church Planting Movements* (Midlothian: WIGTake Resources, 2004)

George, S.K., 'Local-Global Mission: The Cutting Edge', *Missiology: An International Review* (April 2000), 187–97

Gidoomal, R. and M. Wardell, Lions, *Princesses, Gurus: Reaching Your Sikh Neighbour* (Godalming: Highland, 1996)

Gnanakan, K., *The Pluralistic Predicament* (Delhi: ISPCK, 1996)

Green, L., 'Learning To Live and Minister in a Post-Christendom World', *Dawn Report* (February 1998), 5–8

Green, M., *Evangelism in the Early Church* (Toronto: Hodder & Stoughton, 1970)

— (ed.), *Church without Walls: A Global Examination of Cell Church* (Carlisle: Paternoster, 2002)

Grenz, S.J., *A Primer on Postmodernism* (Grand Rapids, MI: W.B. Eerdmans, 1996)

Grys, J., and G. Schaller, 'Growing A Healthy Church', *Ministry* (January 2001), 8–9

Guder, D.L. (ed.), *Missional Church: A Vision for the Sending of the Church in North America* (Grand Rapids, MI: W.B. Eerdmans, 1998)

—, *The Continuing Conversion of the Church* (Grand Rapids, MI: W.B. Eerdmans, 2000)

—, 'Biblical Formation and Discipleship' in L.Y. Barrett et al (eds.), *Treasure in Clay Jars* (Grand Rapids, MI: W.B. Eerdmans, 2004), 59–73

Guthrie, S. 'New Paradigms for Churches and Mission Agencies', *Mission Frontiers* (January–February 2002), 6–8

Hammett, J.S., 'How the Church and Parachurch Should Relate: Arguments for a Servant-Partnership Model', *Missiology: An International Review* (April 2000), 199–207

Hanciles, J.J., 'Migration and Mission: Some Implications for the Twenty-first Century', *International Bulletin of Missionary Research* (October 2003), 146–53

Harrell, D.M., 'Post-Contemporary Worship', *Leadership Journal* (Spring 1999), 37–9

Harris, P., 'Jesus' Followers in the Secular West', *Connections: The Journal of the WEA Missions Commission* (October–December 2003), 20–29

—, 'The World's Students Find a "Mission in Life"', *Evangelical Missions Quarterly* (October 2003), 422–9

Hay, R., 'Reflections from the Younger Generation on Mission and the Great Commission: Are We Dysfunctional, Difficult, or just Different?' *Connections: The Journal of the WEA Missions Commission* (February 2004), 25–32

Hiebert, P.G., *Missiological Implications of Epistemological Shifts: Affirming Truth in a Modern/Postmodern World* (Harrisburg, PA: Trinity, 1999)

Hobbs, 'Dependence on the Holy Spirit' in L.Y. Barrett et al (eds.), *Treasures in Clay Jars* (Grand Rapids, MI: W.B. Eerdmans, 2004), 117–25

Hopkins, B., 'Cell Church: A New Way of Being?' in M. Green (ed.), *Church Without Walls* (Carlisle: Paternoster, 2002), 40–55

Hughes, D., *Castrating Culture: A Christian Perspective on Ethnic Identity from the Margins* (Carlisle: Paternoster Press, 2001)

Huntington, S.P., *The Clash of Civilizations and the Remaking of World Order* (London: Simon & Schuster, 2002)

Jaffarian, M., 'The Demographics of World Religions Entering the Twenty-First Century' in J.J. Bonk (ed.), *Between Past and Future* (Pasadena, CA: William Carey, 2003), 249–71

Jeffrey, T., and S. Chalke, *Connect!* (Carlisle: Authentic Lifestyle, 2003)

Jeffery, T., and R. Johnson, *Churches Going Global: Connect!* 2 (Carlisle: Authentic Lifestyle, 2003)

Jenkins, P., 'The Next Christianity', *The Atlantic Monthly* (October 2002), 53–68

Johnson, R., 'Cutting out the Middleman: Mission and the Local Church in a Globalised, Postmodern World' in R. Tiplady (ed.), *One World or Many?* (Pasadena, CA: William Carey, 2003), 239–50

Johnson, T.M., '"It Can Be Done": The Impact of Modernity and Postmodernity on the Global Mission Plans of Churches and Agencies' in J.J. Bonk (ed.), *Between Past and Future* (Pasadena, CA: William Carey, 2003), 37–49

Johnstone, P., *The Church Is Bigger than You Think* (Bulstrode: Christian Focus Publications/WEC, 1998)

Johnstone, P., and J. Mandryk, *Operation World* (Waynesboro, GA: Paternoster USA, 2001, 6th ed.)

Judge, E., and H. Nugent, 'As Britain Tries To Lure Indian Film-Makers to Leicester', *The Times* (7 February 2004), 4M

Julien, T., 'The Essence of the Church', *Evangelical Missions Quarterly* (April 1998), 148–53

Kaiser, W., *Malachi: God's Unchanging Love* (Grand Rapids, MI: Baker, 1984)

Kane, A., *Let There Be Life* (Basingstoke: Marshall Paperbacks, 1983)

Kenneson, P.D., 'There's No Such Thing as Objective Truth, and It's a Good Thing Too' in T.R. Phillips and D.L. Okholm (eds.), *Christian Apologetics* (Downer's Grove, IL: InterVarsity, 1995), 155–70

Knitter, C., *No Other Name? A Critical Survey of Christian Attitudes Toward World Religions* (Maryknoll, NY: Orbis, 1990)

Kostenberger, A., 'The Contribution of the General Epistles and Revelation to a Biblical Theology of Religions' in E. Rommen and H. Netland (eds.), *Christianity and the Religions* (Pasadena, CA: William Carey, 1995), 113–40

Kraus, C.N., *An Intrusive Gospel: Christian Mission in the Postmodern World* (Downer's Grove, IL: InterVarsity, 1998)

Leader, D., 'The High Price of Erasing Our History', *The Times* (10 April 2004), B3

Lundy, J.D., *We Are the World: Globalisation and the Changing Face of Missions* (Carlisle: OM Publishing, 1999)

—, *Servant Leadership for Slow Learners* (Carlisle: Authentic Lifestyle, 2002)

—, 'Multiculturalism and Pluralisation: Kissing Cousins of Globalisation' in R. Tiplady (ed.), *One World or Many?* (Pasadena, CA: William Carey, 2003), 71–84

Marazano, L., 'The Unreached – Right on Your Campus', *Mission Frontiers* (September 2001), 30–31

McGrath, A., 'Conclusion: A Particularist View' in D.L. Okholm. and T.R. Phillips (eds.), *More Than One Way?* (Grand Rapids, MI: Zondervan, 1995), 200–209

McLaren, B.D., *The Church on the Other Side: Doing Mission in the Postmodern Matrix* (Grand Rapids, MI: Zondervan, 2000)

McNeal, R., *A Work of Heart: Understanding How God Shapes Spiritual Leaders* (San Francisco, CA: Jossey-Bass, 2000)

Middleton, J.R., and B.J. Walsh, 'Facing the Postmodern Scalpel' in T.R. Philips and D.L. Okholm (eds.), *Christian Apologetics* (Downer's Grove, IL: InterVarsity, 1995), 131–54

Miley, G., *Loving the Church, Blessing the Nations: Pursuing the Role of Local Churches in Global Mission* (Waynesboro, GA: Gabriel, 2003)

Minear, P.S., *Images of the Church in the New Testament* (Philadelphia, PA: The Westminster Press, 1960)

Moerman, M. (ed.), *Transforming Our Nation: Empowering the Canadian Church to a Greater Harvest* (Richmond: Church Leadership, 1998)

Moreau, A.S., 'Religious Borrowing as a Two-Way Street: An Introduction to Animistic Tendencies on the Euro-North American Context' in E. Rommen and H. Netland (eds.), *Christianity and the Religions* (Pasadena, CA: William Carey, 1995), 166–83

Moreau, A.S., and M. O'Rear, 'All You Ever Wanted on Short-term Mission', *Evangelical Missions Quarterly* (January 2004), 100–104

Morris, L., *1 and 2 Thessalonians* (Leicester: Inter-Varsity, 1983)

Motz, A., *Reclaiming a Nation: The Challenge of Re-evangelizing Canada by the Year 2000* (Richmond: Church Leadership, 1990)

Muck, T., *Alien Gods on American Turf* (Wheaton, IL: Victor, 1990)

Murray, S., *Post-Christendom* (Carlisle: Paternoster Press, 2004)

Myers, B.L., *Walking With the Poor* (Maryknoll, NY: Orbis Books, 1999)

Neill, S., *A History of Christian Missions* (Middlesex: Penguin, 1975)

Netland, H., 'Application: Mission in a Pluralistic World' in E. Rommen and H. Netland (eds.), *Christianity and the Religions* (Pasadena, CA: William Carey, 1995), 254–69

Newbigin, L., *The Gospel in a Pluralistic Society* (Grand Rapids, MI: W.B. Eerdmans, 1994)

—, *The Open Secret: An Introduction to the Theology of Mission* (Grand Rapids, MI: W.B. Eerdmans, 1995, 2nd ed.)

Okholm, D.L., and T.R. Phillips (eds.), *More Than One Way? Four Views on Salvation in a Pluralistic World* (Grand Rapids, MI: Zondervan, 1995)

Ohmae, K., *The Borderless World: Power and Strategy in the Interlinked Economy* (New York, NY: Harper Business, 1990)

Parrott, D., 'Managing the Short-Term Missions Explosion', *Evangelical Missions Quarterly* (July 2004), 356–60

Phillips, T.R., and D.L. Okholm (eds.), *Christian Apologetics in the Postmodern World* (Downer's Grove, IL: InterVarsity, 1995)

Pinnock, C., *A Wideness in a God's Mercy* (Grand Rapids, MI: Zondervan, 1992)

Piper, J., *Let the Nations Be Nations: The Supremacy of God in Mission* (Grand Rapids, MI: Baker, 1996)

Plueddemann, J., 'Church and Mission Together', *World Pulse* (26 September 2003), 6–7

Plueddemann, C. and J., 'In Praise of Long-Term Missionaries', *World Pulse* (4 June 2004), 8

Po, M., 'God's Creative Mission for Lay Professionals', *Missiology: An International Review* (January 2004), 57–69

Postman, N., *Amusing Ourselves to Death: Public Discourse in the Age of Show Business* (New York, NY: Penguin Books, 1985)

Poston, L., 'Christianity as a Minority Religion' in E. Rommen and H. Netland (eds.), *Christianity and the Religions* (Pasadena, CA: William Carey, 1995), 218–38

Ramachandra, V., *Gods That Fail: Modern Idolatry and Christian Mission* (Carlisle: Paternoster, 1996)

—, 'Global Society: Challenge for Christian Mission', *Anvil* (Vol. 21, No. 1, 2004), 9–21

Reesor, L., 'What Kind of Church Will It Take?' *Mission Frontiers* (December 2000), 23–4

Reissner, A., 'The Dance of Partnership: A Theological Reflection', *Missiology: An International Review* (January 2001), 3–10

Ripley, D.L., 'Reaching the World at our Doorstep', *Evangelical Missions Quarterly* (April 1994), 142–50

Rommen, E., and H. Netland (eds.), *Christianity and the Religions: A Biblical Theology of World Religions* (Pasadena, CA: William Carey, 1995)

Ross, K.R., '"Blessed Reflex": Mission as God's Spiral of Renewal', *International Bulletin of Missionary Research* (October 2003), 162–8

sam.george@sbcglobal.net, personal communication, 11 November 2004

Schmidt, K., '"Missional" Churches Seek to Personalize Global Outreach', *World Pulse* (3 November 2000), 1–2

Seim, B. (ed.), *Canada's New Harvest: Helping Churches Touch Newcomers* (Toronto: SIM, 1999, 2nd ed.)

—, 'A 10/40 Twist', *Seedbed* (Fall 2003), 13–6

Severn, F.M., 'Mission Societies: Are They Biblical?' *Evangelical Missions Quarterly* (July 2000), 320–26

Shigematu, K., 'Transitioning to Future Reality', unpublished paper delivered at the 'Multicultural Church Conference' in Toronto, 2002

Smith, G.T., 'Religions and the Bible: An Agenda for Evangelicals' in E. Rommen and H. Netland (eds.), *Christianity and the Religions* (Pasadena, CA: William Carey, 1995), 9–29

Stackhouse, M. (ed.), *The Local Church in a Global Era* (Cambridge, UK: W.B. Eerdmans, 2000)

Stevens, R.P., *Liberating the Laity: Equipping All the Saints for Ministry* (Downer's Grove, IL: InterVarsity, 1985)

Stoner, D., 'The Missional Church Is Passionately "Glocal"', *Connections: The Journal of the WEA Missions Committee* (February 2004), 51–5

Taber, J., and C. Clark, 'Key Martin Aids Debate June Election', *The Toronto Star* (20 April 2004), A1

Telford, T., *Missions in the 21st Century: Getting Your Church into the Game* (Wheaton, IL: Harold Shaw, 1998)

Thomas, T.V., *Mobilizing a Church on the Move: The Diaspora in Mission* (Toronto: TIM Centre, 1998)

Tidball, D., *The Social Context of the New Testament* (Carlisle: Paternoster, 2003)

Tiplady, R. (ed.), *PostMission* (Carlisle: Paternoster, 2002)

— (ed.), *One World or Many? The Impact of Globalisation on Mission* (Pasadena, CA: William Carey, 2003)

—, *World of Difference: Global Mission at the Pic 'N' Mix Counter* (Carlisle: Paternoster, 2003)

Valerio, R., 'Globalisation and Economics: A World Gone Bananas' in R. Tiplady (ed.), *One World or Many?* (Pasadena, CA: William Carey, 2003), 13–32

Van Engen, C., *God's Missionary People: Rethinking the Purpose of the Local Church* (Grand Rapids, MI: Baker, 1995)

—, 'Toward a Theology of Mission Partnerships', *Missiology: An International Review* (January 2001), 11–44

Ward, P., *Liquid Church* (Carlisle: Paternoster, 2002)

Warren, R., *The Purpose Driven Church: Growth without Compromising Your Message & Mission* (Grand Rapids, MI: Zondervan, 1995)

White, J., *The Church and the Parachurch: Uneasy Marriage* (Portland, OR: Multnomah, 1983)

Willmer, K.W., and J.D. Schmidt, *The Prospering Parachurch: Enlarging the Boundaries of God's Kingdom* (San Francisco, CA: Jossey-Bass, 1998)

Winter, R., 'The Two Structures of God's Redemptive Mission,' *Missiology: An International Review* (January 1974), 121–39

World Pulse, 'So What Can We Expect To Find?' (21 November 2003)

www.bramaleabaptist.org (last accessed 10 November 2004)

www.mhbcml.org (last accessed 21 September 2004)

www.new-life-church.org.uk (last accessed 9 January 2005)

www.nike.com/europe (last accessed 17 October 2004)

www.usnews.com/issue050110/usnews/10muslims.htm (last accessed 4 January 2005)

www.what4.org.uk/motiv8 (last accessed 1 June 2005)

Yancey, P., *Reaching for the Invisible God: What Can We Expect To Find?* (Grand Rapids, MI: Zondervan, 2000)

Zeimer, D.A., 'Practices That Demonstrate God's Intent for the World' in L.Y Barrett et al (eds.), *Treasures in Clay Jars* (Grand Rapids, MI: W.B. Eerdmans: 2004), 84–99

Zoba, W.M., 'Are Christians Prepared for Muslims in the Mainstream?' *Christianity Today* (3 April 2000), 40–50

Notes

Introduction

1 Warren, *Purpose Driven Church*, 32.
2 A metanarrative is a 'totalizing claim about reality' or a 'large-scale interpretation of the whole of history with purportedly universal application': Middleton and Walsh, 'Postmodern Scalpel', 139.
3 Murray, *Post-Christendom*, 1.
4 An excellent article explicating the view that 'narrow is the way' and that the church should never expect to be statistically in the majority is Poston's 'Christianity is a Minority Religion', 218–38.
5 Martin Kahler, as quoted in Bosch, *Transforming Mission*, 16.
6 Murray, *Post-Christendom*, 86–7.
7 Callahan, *Church Leadership*, 3.
8 McNeal, *A Work of Heart*, 90.
9 Green, 'Learning to Live', 8.
10 Lundy, 'Multiculturalism', 72.
11 Hopkins, 'Cell Church', 43.
12 Ohmae, *The Borderless World*.
13 Ward, *Liquid Church*, 2–3.
14 Freidman, *Lexus*, 61.
15 Lundy, *We Are the World*.
16 Guder (ed.), *Missional Church*, 158.
17 Unless otherwise mentioned, the *New International Version* of the Bible is the one used.
18 I am indebted to Yancey's use of the Rosetta stone as an illustration, if differently, in *Reaching for the Invisible God*, 139.
19 Clowney, 'Biblical Models of the Church', 85, 105; cf. Minear, *Images of the Church* for the same conclusion but a complete coverage of the 96 NT images of the church.

Chapter 1

1 Guder (ed.), *Missional Church*, 4.
2 Ramachandra, *Gods That Fail*, 58–9.
3 Newbigin, *The Open Secret*, 70.
4 Bosch, *Transforming Mission*, 1, 228, 257; for a perceptive discussion of this trinitaritan theology of mission, see Bjork, 'Trinitarian Understanding', 231–44.
5 Beckham, 'The Church with Two Wings', 31; cf. Ward, *Liquid Church*, 49–55 for another thoughtful reflection on the Trinity mirroring how church should perceive her purpose and function.
6 Bosch, *Transforming Mission*, 372.
7 Newbigin, *Pluralistic Society*, 231.
8 ibid., 64.
9 ibid., 17.
10 Callahan, *Church Leadership*, 60.
11 Murray, *Post-Christendom*, 305.
12 Guder, *Missional Church*, 72.
13 Newbigin, *Pluralistic Society*, 227.
14 Guder, *Continuing Conversion*, 155.
15 Jeffery and Johnson
16 Douglas, 'Globalization', 205.
17 Bosch, *Transforming Mission*, 403–8.
18 Callahan, *Church Leadership*, 31.
19 Guder, *Continuing Conversion*, 129.
20 Bonhoeffer, 166.
21 Callahan, *Church Leadership*, 21.

Chapter 2

1 Jeffery and Chalke, *Connect!* 9.
2 *Majority world* is the term we will use to refer to those who have popularly been categorized as coming from the *two-thirds world*, that is, from the continental groupings of peoples in Africa, Asia, Latin America, and Oceania, hitherto and pejoratively labelled as *developing world*, and until recent decades making up about two-thirds of the world's population. Realizing it is unfair to generalize (in this case distinguishing certain cultures and nations from those found in the *western world*), it nevertheless is helpful to make this distinction in that people from these continents tend to have a psychic bond forged out of common historical experiences such

as their being colonized. *Majority world* is increasingly being used by missiologists to refer to such people.

3 Zoba, 'Are Christians Prepared', 40.
4 www.usnews.com/usnews/issue/050110/usnews/10muslims. htm
5 Bremner, 'Stoned to Death', 55.
6 Amiel, 'France'.
7 Cited in Gidoomal and Wardell, *Lions*, 8.
8 ibid., 15.
9 Judge and Nugent, 'Indian Film-Makers', M3.
10 Seim, 'A 10/40 Twist', 13–4.
11 *World Pulse*, 'What Can We Expect?' 2.
12 Jenkins, 'The Next Christianity', 59.
13 Thomas, *Mobilizing*, 2.
14 R. Gwyn quoted in Seim, *Canada's New Harvest*, 96.
15 Adeney, 'Is God Colorblind or Colorful?', 89.
16 Muck, *Alien Gods*, 28.
17 Bjork, 'Foreign Missions',17.
18 Ripley, 'Reaching the World', 143.
19 Couto, 'Multicultural Diversity', 3.
20 Carson, *Gagging of God*, 14.
21 T. Clegg and W. Bird quoted in Fuder, 'Students', 4.
22 Moerman, *Transforming Our Nation*, 344.
23 Bailey, 'Mission Field', 54.
24 Aganon, 'An International Family Affair', 10.
25 Statistics in an email from sam.george@sbcglobal.net
26 Marazano, 'The Unreached', 31.
27 Couto, 'Reaching Immigrants', 44.
28 Seim, *Canada's New Harvest*, 34.
29 Seim, 'A 10/40 Twist', 15.
30 ibid.
31 Browne, 'Churches Revived', 28.
32 Hughes, *Castrating Culture*, 126.
33 Telford, *Missions*, 55.
34 Bonk, 'Thinking Small', 154.

Chapter 3

1 Quoted in Ramachandra, 'Global Society', 15.
2 Erickson, *Truth*, 9 distinguishes between *postmodernism* and *postmodernity* as 'the former is the intellectual beliefs of a specific

period while the latter is the cultural phenomenon thereof.' It is *postmodernity* that we are interested in relating to particularly while interfacing with the church's witness in the twenty-first century.

3 Jean-Francois Lyotard and Zygmunt Bauman quoted in Tiplady, *Postmission*, 58.

4 Tiplady argues that the roots of postmodernity were laid in the European religious wars of the 1600s, such as the Thirty Years War when Protestant and Roman Catholic countries devastated one another, in *World of Difference*, 27–8.

5 Quoted in Middleton and Walsh, 'Postmodern Scalpel', 139.

6 An example of one such excellent survey is Grenz, *A Primer on Postmodernism*.

7 Leader, 'High Price', 3.

8 Dylhoff, 'Generation X', 448.

9 Carson, *Gagging of God*, 19–22.

10 Cited in Colson, *The Body*, 247.

11 Hiebert, *Missiological Implications*, 38–42.

12 Quoted in Carson, *Gagging of God*, 43.

13 Erickson, *Truth*, 290–91.

14 Some Christian denominations and theologians are closet or open pluralists, an example of the latter being Knitter, *No Other Name?*

15 Smith, 'Religions', 10.

16 This is not the view held by this author who believes that the Bible teaches *religious exclusivism*, but 'evangelical' examples of the proponents of *religious inclusivism* include well-known theologians like Pinnock, *Wideness*.

17 Carson, *Gagging of God*, 33; cf. Murray, *Post-Christendom*, 235.

18 Craig, 'Politically Incorrect Salvation', 82.

19 British comedian, Stephen Fry, quoted in Ward, *Liquid Church*, 56.

20 Netland, 'Application', 257.

21 Coupland, *Generation X*, 163.

22 Tiplady, *World of Difference*, 26–7.

23 Motz, *Reclaiming a Nation*, 285.

24 Colson, 'Salad-Bar Christianity', 80.

25 Moreau, 'Religious Borrowing', 172–3.

26 Murray, *Post-Christendom*, 13.

27 Generation X refers to those born between 1965 and 1979 and Millennium or Generation Y people as those born 1980 and later, now just emerging into adulthood in some cases.

28 Craig, 'Politically Incorrect Salvation', 78.

29 Tiplady, *World of Difference*, 31–40.

30 Warren, *Purpose Driven Church*, 200.

31 Dawn, *Reaching Out*, 27–8.
32 Phillips and Okholm, *Christian Apologetics*, 13.
33 Guder, *Missional Church*, 35.
34 Carson, *Gagging of God*, 49.
35 Dawn, *Reaching Out* 18.
36 ibid., 23.
37 Carson, *Gagging of God*, 45.
38 ibid., 48.
39 Hiebert, *Missiological Implications*, 53.
40 Cited in Tiplady, *Postmission*, 70.
41 Hiebert, *Missiological Implications*, 45; cf. Erickson, *Truth or Consequences*, 231–3.
42 Dawn, *Reaching Out*, 49.
43 Dylhoff, 'Generation X', 450.

Chapter 4

1 Neill, *History*, 44; Murray, *Post Christendom*, 28, estimates a growth rate of 40 per cent per decade for the first 250 years.
2 Green, *Early Church*, 13–4.
3 ibid., 16.
4 ibid., 43.
5 Carson, *Gagging of God*, 487.
6 Green, *Early Church*, 34–7.
7 Quoted in Tidball, *Social Context*, 66–7.
8 Kostenberger, 'General Epistles and Revelation', 132.
9 ibid. 86–7, 183.
10 ibid. 88.
11 Quoted in Stevens, *Liberating the Laity*, 22.
12 Camp, 'Local Church's Involvement', 208.
13 ibid., 61.
14 Green, *Early Church*, 18.
15 ibid., 39.
16 ibid., 40.
17 Bosch, *Transforming Mission*, 48.
18 Green, *Early Church*, 41.
19 Guder, *Missional Church*, 128.
20 Camp 'Local Church's Involvement', 207–8; cf. Green, *Early Church*, 188–93.
21 Cited in Bosch, *Transforming Mission*, 49.
22 Fouch, 'Globalization', 125.

23 ibid., 206.
24 Murray, *Post-Christendom*, 217; cf. Bosch, *Transforming Mission*, 472–3.
25 Morris, *1 and 2 Thessalonians*, 38.
26 Green, *Early Church*, 194; Tidball, *Social Context*, 82.

Chapter 5

1 Taber and Clark, 'Key Martin Aids Debate June Election', A1.
2 Carson, *Gagging of God*, 35.
3 Green, *Church without Walls*, 47.
4 Dylhoff, 'Generation X', 448.
5 Callahan, *Church Leadership*, 106.
6 Dawn, *Reaching Out*, 125, 168.
7 Guder, *Missional Church*, 41.
8 ibid., 164.
9 Miley, *Loving the Church*, 24.
10 Dawn, *Reaching Out*, 76.
11 Ward, *Liquid Church*, 76.
12 Dawn, *Reaching Out*, 90.
13 Warren, *Purpose Driven Church*, 242. John Piper makes 'missions exists because worship doesn't' his battle cry in numerous books, like *Let the Nations Be Glad: The Supremacy of God in Mission*.
14 Harell, 'Post-Contemporary Worship', 39.
15 Lundy, *Servant Leadership*, 178–97.
16 Po, 'God's Creative Mission', 60.
17 Guder, *Continuing Conversion*, 111.
18 Tracing the wide usage of *laos* and its various meanings in the *LXX* of the OT and its 141 uses in the NT is Bietenhard, 'People', 788–805.
19 Stevens, *Liberating the Laity*, 22.
20 ibid., 32.
21 Warren, *Purpose Driven Church*, 103–9.
22 I have separate chapters on these two qualities in *Servant Leadership for Slow Learners*, chapters 3 and 5 respectively.
23 Tiplady, *Postmission*, 18.
24 Dylhoff, 'Generation X', 447–8.
25 Bosch, *Transforming Mission*, 84.
26 A comprehensive apologetic for *transformational development* in mission is found in B. Myers, *Walking with the Poor* (Monrovia: MARC, 1999).

27 Fouch, 'Globalization', 128.

28 Galadima, 'Future of Christianity', 200.

29 I am not inferring that topical or thematic preaching is spiritual junk food or that all expositional preaching is good.

30 Dawn, *Reaching Out*, 206.

31 Guder, *Missional Church*, 40–41.

32 Adelphi and Hahn, *The Integrity of the Bible*, 13–27.

33 Erickson, *Truth*, 301–2; cf. Hiebert, *Missiological Implications*, 101–3.

34 Carson, *Gagging of God*, 103.

35 Bosch, *Transforming Mission*, 186–7.

36 Gnanakan, *Pluralistic Predicament*, 153. Ward's *Liquid Church* similarly provides a positive starting point in dealing with non-Christians instead of assuming the worst about them, essential to an effective outreach strategy today.

37 There are several excellent evangelical treatments of the uniqueness of Christ in relation to other religions, including Daniel Clendenin's, *Many Gods, Many Lords*.

38 McGrath, 'Conclusion', 208.

39 Craig, 'Politically Incorrect Salvation', 76–7.

40 Bosch, *Transforming Mission*, 483.

41 Gnanakan, *Pluralistic Predicament*, 162.

42 Kraus, *An Intrusive Gospel*, 26.

43 Fernando, *The Christian's Attitude*, 172.

44 Carson, *Gagging of God*, 349.

45 Zeimer, 'Practices', 93.

46 Tiplady, *Postmission*, 10.

47 Fernando, *The Christian's Attitude*, 29–32.

48 Newbigin, *Pluralistic Society*, 14.

49 Kenneson, 'No Such Thing', 166–7.

50 Newbigin, *Pluralistic Society*, 99.

Chapter 6

1 Much of the material of this chapter, unless otherwise noted, is gleaned through visiting the church for a weekend, the written materials collected there, information gathered from the church's website, and in various conversations with Keith Sparzak, especially in an interview recorded in January 2004.

2 Critiqued in Grys and Schaller, 'Growing a Healthy Church', 8.

3 Stoner, 'Passionately "Glocal"', 51–2.

4 Warren, *Purpose Driven Church*, 51.

5 Stoner, 'Passionately "Glocal"', 53.

6 North Africa is considered to be made up of the five Arab and Berber Muslim countries, namely, Mauritania, Morocco, Algeria, Tunisia, and Libya.

7 Stoner, 'Passionately "Glocal"', 53.

8 Beckham, 'The Church with Two Wings', 30.

9 Stoner, 'Passionately "Glocal"', 52.

10 ibid., 53.

11 ibid., 54.

12 I should note here that the church's political advocacy for the stateless Sahrawi is considered by Darrell Guder, missional church proponent, as the sort of pursuit of justice on behalf of the disenfranchised that is one of the hallmarks of missionality in a local church in *Continuing Conversion*, 124.

13 Tiplady, *Postmission*, 76.

14 Those older baby boomers (born between 1946 and 1964 according to sociologists) and veterans (born 1909–45) who are looking to give remaining productive years to cross-cultural service are often called 'builders' in mission circles.

15 Guder, *Continuing Conversion*, 178.

Chapter 7

1 97 per cent of people inhabiting the least evangelized countries live in the rectangular-shaped window popularized in the 1990s as the 10/40 Window by the AD2000 & Beyond Movement, 'the window extend[ing] from West Africa to East Asia, from 10 degrees north to forty degrees north of the equator'; *10/40 Window*.

2 Some of these illustrations have been adapted from Borthwick, 'Mobilizing the Next Generation', 434–42.

3 Valerio, 'Globalisation and Economics', 21.

4 Harris, 'Jesus' Followers', 22–4.

5 Stated in a Lausanne Forum lecture in Toronto by Stephen Foster in 2000, 'The Impatience of the Mission Agency with the Local Church'.

6 Jaffarian, 'Demographics', 262.

7 Jeffery and Chalke, *Connect!*, 42.

8 McLaren, *The Church on the Other Side*, 122.

9 He made the same comment over lunch with me in London in July 2004.

10 We define *unreached people group* as *a people that does not have a viable indigenous community of believing Christians with adequate numbers of resources to evangelize their own people without outside, or cross-cultural, assistance* as defined in Johnstone and Mandryk, *Operation World*, 759.
11 Newbigin, *Pluralistic Society*, 121.
12 Johnson, '"It Can Be Done"', 47.
13 Recent analyses have shown that the predictions that majority world missionaries would outnumber western world missionaries by the year 2000 were unfounded.
14 Johnstone, *The Church Is Bigger than You Think*, 138.
15 McLaren, *The Church on the Other Side*, 128–9.
16 C. and J. Plueddemann, 'Long-Term Missionaries', 8. From parachurch agencies alone, the number of Americans going on short-term mission trips grew from 97,272 in 1998 to 346,270 in 2001, an amazing 256 per cent increase in three years: Moreau and O'Rear, 'Short-Term Mission', 100. Churches send out directly the vast number of those going on short-term mission trips, hence the Plueddemanns' claim.
17 Parrott, 'Missions Explosion', 357.
18 ibid.
19 Miley, *Loving the Church*, 49.
20 Parrott, 'Missions Explosion', 358.
21 Harris, 'Jesus' Followers', 24.
22 McLaren, *The Church on the Other Side*, 123.
23 Coupland, *Generation X*, 28.
24 Harris, 'The World's Students', 422–3, 429.
25 Hay, 'Reflections', 31.
26 ibid., 31–2.
27 Dylhoff, 'Generation X', 449.

Chapter 8

1 Kane, *Let There Be Life*, 104.
2 www.new-life-church.org.uk
3 Telford, *Missions*, 159.
4 Kane, *Let There Be Life*, 52.

Chapter 9

1 Willmer and Schmidt, *Prospering Parachurch*, xii.
2 Guthrie, 'Paradigms', 6.

3 Winter 'Two Structures', 121–39.

4 Bosch, *Transforming Mission*, 328.

5 Cited in Willmer and Schmidt, *Prospering Parachurch*, 13.

6 White, *The Church and the Parachurch*, 64.

7 For a fuller examination of this issue and passage see Joseph and Michele C., 'Field-Governed Mission Structures Part I: In the New Testament', 59–64.

8 Bosch, *Transforming Mission*, 378–9.

9 Severn, 'Mission Societies', 323.

10 Cited in Camp, 'Local Church's Involvement', 231.

11 Guder, *Missional Church*, 75.

12 Willmer and Schmidt, *Prospering Parachurch*, 171.

13 ibid., 10.

14 ibid., 52.

15 Tiplady, *World of Difference*, 91.

16 Johnson, 'Cutting Out the Middleman', 240.

17 Willmer and Schmidt, *Prospering Parachurch*, 193–4.

18 Baker, 'William Carey', 193.

19 Willmer and Schmidt, *Prospering Parachurch*, 171.

20 Tiplady makes this point strongly in *World of Difference*, 90.

21 ibid., 110.

22 Callahan, *Church Leadership*, 154–5.

23 OT scholar and president of Gordon-Conwell Theological Seminary, Walter Kaiser, in his commentary on Malachi, *Malachi: God's Unchanging Love*, 92–3, in examining the term, *storehouse*, found 80 times in the OT, concludes his study by saying, 'Accordingly, we must be careful about using this verse to insist on "storehouse tithing" by which some require that *all* giving to God's work must be channelled through the local church! We must indeed "bring" the tithes, but in fairness to the text, the "storehouse" is not equated with the local church.'

24 Johnstone, *The Church Is Bigger than You Think*, 186.

25 Guthrie, 'Paradigms', 7.

26 ibid.

27 Foster, 'The Impatience of the Mission Agency with the Local Church', 7.

28 Borthwick, 'Mobilizing the Next Generation', 440–41.

29 Plueddemann, 'Church and Mission Together', 6.

30 Tiplady, *Postmission*, 76; *World of Difference*, 123–9.

31 Van Engen, 'Toward a Theology of Mission Partnerships', 12–14.

32 Hammett, 'Church and Parachurch', 200.

Chapter 10

1 Quotes of Bramalea staff not supported by a footnote come out of a two hour interview I conducted with the senior pastor, the glocal discipleship pastor, the worship pastor, the chairman of the board, and the interim pastor of counselling.
2 WASP is a Canadian expression meaning 'White Anglo Saxon Protestant'.
3 Bramalea Baptist Church, *Let's Talk! Our Church Family Newsletter*, 1.
4 ibid.
5 Guder, *Continuing Conversion*, 69.
6 Seim, *Canada's New Harvest*, 13.
7 Hughes, *Castrating Culture*, 16ff. makes much the same point.
8 Warren, *Purpose Driven Church*, 201.

Chapter 11

1 The name *Thy Kingdom Come* and the country *Lostland* are pseudonyms for a real church in a 'restricted access country' (countries not offering missionary visas by and large). To protect the church and her ministry, anything that would put the church at risk has been intentionally disguised. Nevertheless the description of the church is not fictitious.
2 Much of the material for this chapter was gleaned through a two-hour interview with the mission pastor, whom we shall call Pastor Paul, the church website, and the aforementioned personal visit.
3 Stevens, *Liberating the Laity*, 105.
4 Hobbs, 'Dependence', 118.

Chapter 12

1 Julien, 'Essence', 152.
2 Guder, *Continuing Conversion*, 199, 207.
3 Schmidt, '"Missional" Churches', 1.
4 Warren, *Purpose Driven Church*, 138–9.
5 Murray, *Post-Christendom*, 255.
6 Newbigin, *Pluralistic Society*, 127.
7 Moerman, *Transforming Our Nation*, 103.
8 Garrison, *Church Planting Movements*.

9 Murray, *Post-Christendom*, 254, 257.

10 ibid., 275.

11 Reissner, 'Dance', 5–6.

12 A Barna poll cited in Harris, 'Jesus' Followers', 23–4.

13 Murray, *Post-Christendom*, 228.

14 ibid., 230.

15 Ross, '"Blessed Reflex"', 164.

16 George, 'Local-Global Mission', 194.

17 Harris, 'Jesus' Followers', 25.

18 This thesis is fully developed in S.P. Huntington's seminal work, *The Clash of Civilizations and the Remaking of World Order*.

19 Guder, 'Biblical Formation, 46, 74.

20 Ramachandra, 'Global Society', 21.

21 Newbigin, *Pluralistic Society*, 137; cf. Murray, *Post-Christendom*, 235–9.

22 McNeal, *A Work of Heart*, 102.

23 Van Engen, *God's Missionary People*, 111.

24 This illustration comes from J. Collins, *Good to Great*, 90–91, but is applied in a different way.